ADAM MABRY

THE ART OF REST

FAITH TO HIT PAUSE
IN A WORLD THAT
NEVER STOPS

thegoodbook
COMPANY

Published by
The Good Book Company
Tel (UK): 0333 123 0880
International: +44 (0) 208 942 0880
Email: info@thegoodbook.co.uk

Websites:
North America: www.thegoodbook.com
UK: www.thegoodbook.co.uk
Australia: www.thegoodbook.com.au
New Zealand: www.thegoodbook.co.nz

Design by André Parker

ISBN: 9781784983208 | Printed in the UK

"How fascinating to read a book about one of the greatest challenges of our time, written by a man who once failed miserably in the face of that challenge. In these pages, Adam Mabry gives us what we most need—a vision of rest tethered to God, rooted in the practical, and shot through with a humorous understanding of our work-addicted folly. This book is a gift!"

STEPHEN MANSFIELD, *New York Times* bestselling author; host of the Stephen Mansfield Podcast

"This little jewel of a book made my heart sing. Like most of us, Adam Mabry has struggled with the modern tyranny of busyness. In this short book—easily readable even by the busiest—he shows the biblical principle of rest to be a gift of grace, a taste of heaven, and a counter-cultural statement of trust in our heavenly Father. An inspiring and challenging read!"

CLARE HEATH-WHYTE, author of *Old Wives' Tales* and *Everyone a Child Should Know*

"I have to admit, it made me laugh when I heard Adam was writing a book on rest. Adam is one of the hardest-working people I know, and he seems to have endless energy—but that might be why he is the perfect person to write on this topic. He is a gifted writer with an important message for everyone—rest is a gift that God wants you to enjoy. I pray that this book inspires you to learn the art of rest."

STEVE MURRELL, President, Every Nation Churches & Ministries; founding pastor, Victory Church, Manila, Philippines

"In this excellent book, Adam Mabry shows us that rest for the Christian is not optional—it's commanded for our good. After a careful handling of a biblical theology of rest, Mabry applies God's good command in a gospel-saturated and realistic way. This book will do you good and enable you to rest well in a restless world."

ROBIN WEEKES, Minister, Emmanuel Church, Wimbledon, UK

"*The Art of Rest* was itself a welcome rest to this retired theologian living in Florida (the outro in this book will enable you to appreciate the reference). I disagree with Adam somewhat about the Fourth Commandment, but he is wonderfully right about, as he says, 96% of what the Bible says on rest. His writing is rich, clear, conversational, and vivid. It's as if he, Adam, were right there with you as you read. And Adam calls us to a lifestyle enabled by God's grace in Jesus, in which we can find rest in work as well as rest away from work."

DR. JOHN FRAME, Professor of Systematic Theology & Philosophy, Reformed Theological Seminary, Orlando, Florida

"Nobody teaches us to rest. Adam Mabry—like many others—discovered the consequences the hard way. This 'starter in the art of rest' explores why we find it hard to stop, and makes an urgent plea for us to discover patterns and rhythms of rest before the pace and complexity of life overwhelm us. This is a book I really wish I had read when I was starting in Christian ministry."

MARCUS HONEYSETT, Director, Living Leadership; author of *Fruitful Leaders*

"We in the 24/7 world of the West have forgotten why—and how—to rest. As a result, we're over-extended and sleep-deprived. Our relationships are strained, our bodies suffer stress-induced disorders, and worst of all, our worship of God is superficial. We need help. And Adam Mabry's book is a great help. Here we get to the heart of the problem and then find very helpful recommendations for recovering the lost art of rest."

JON BLOOM, co-founder, Desiring God; author of *Not By Sight*

"Read this to gain insight into the purpose behind the pillars of sabbath with which God architected man's soul. If you are allergic to conviction, read this book with your favorite antihistamine close by."

BRETT FULLER, Pastor, Grace Covenant Church, Chantilly, Virginia; North American Director, Every Nation Churches & Ministries; Chaplain, Washington Redskins

"What a refreshing book! With surprising authenticity, delightful humor, and profound biblical insight, Adam Mabry has given Christians a gift... and a gift that will last a lifetime. It's not a book you just read; it's a book to which you will refer often and that over a lifetime. I'm an old guy and just wish that I had read this book when I was younger. But still, this book is a life-changer even for an old guy 'cramming for finals.' My life is going to be richer and better because of *The Art of Rest*. Yours will be too. Read it and give it to everyone you know!"

STEVE BROWN, *New York Times* bestselling author; host of *Steve Brown, Etc.* and *Key Life*; Professor, Reformed Theological, Orlando and Knox Seminary, Fort Lauderdale, Florida

"I know this message is disruptive because it interrupts the auto-pilot default life-styles that we have taken for granted. I also know the messenger/author and what a difference practicing rest has made to him. His radical change gives me hope that leaders can lead from a place of rest, and the results are so much more sustainable."

DR. JOSEPH UMIDI, Executive Vice President, Regent University

"*The Art of Rest* isn't just about rest; it's about life—what we are here for. Adam Mabry brings together personal experience, biblical conviction, and keen cultural analysis into a brief and enjoyable book that offers a gospel-centered solution to an ever-present problem. I needed this book. I think you probably do, too."

TREVIN WAX, Director for Bibles and Reference, LifeWay Christian Resources; author of *This is our Time* and *Eschatalogical Discipleship*

"I've read a lot of books on rest for busy Christians, but this is one of the best. It's lively, convicting, and relentlessly focused on Jesus."

COLLIN HANSEN, Editorial Director, The Gospel Coalition

*To the teachers, parents, friends,
and family who've paused to help me.
Thank you.*

CONTENTS

Intro: I Don't Do Rest   11

1 A Bit of Art History   23

2 Rest Allows Remembering   41

3 Rest Is Resistance   59

4 Rest Restores Relationship   77

5 Rest Brings Reward   95

6 Starting to Stop   111

Outro: Lessons Learned in Florida   125

Bibliography   137

INTRO:
I DON'T DO REST

When I told my wife that I'd started writing a book on rest, she laughed at me.

And it wasn't a chuckle, but a hearty belly-laugh—the laugh of someone who has just heard something hilarious and who can't quite contain how ironic and unlikely what they've just heard is.

This whole situation—me writing a book on rest—is even more ironic than Alanis Morissette's song "Ironic" being filled with situations that aren't actually ironic. There are two reasons for the laughter emanating from the other half of my marriage about the book that you're now reading: one unserious, but the other very serious indeed.

UNLIKELY MESSENGER

There used to be a regular argument in my house almost every Saturday. I'm a pastor, so Saturdays are my day off. And we'd celebrate like this...

After bringing my wife, Hope, her morning coffee, I'd ask her something like, "So, honey, what would you like to do today?"

"Oh, I don't know. Let's just be relaxed," she'd reply, quite sweetly, contentedly holding her coffee.

"OK cool," I would fire back. "So... how would you like to do that?"

"I don't know. Let's just hang out," she'd say, nonchalantly.

My heart-rate would then increase, eyebrows raised to hint at the flicker of anxiety inside.

"OK. Well, how exactly would you like to 'just hang out?'"

I'd then proceed with a list of activities which I thought were conducive to this "just hanging out" of which she spoke. We could take a walk, play a game, have a discussion... any of these. But please, PLEASE, could we have a plan for our relaxation, because the whole day could go by without us making progress on that "hanging out" task, and then we would end up failing to hit our goal of relaxing.

Looking up from her coffee, she would then say something like, "Adam, I don't know how I want to hang out. Let's just relax."

She'd smile at me, because to her what she'd just said made perfect sense. But my face would twist slightly, and frustration would well up within me, and as I replied to her, some—well, most—of that frustration would leak out through my words and my tone... and our regularly scheduled day-off dust-up would get underway.

And that would mark the end of any relaxing.

Here's my problem.

I don't "just hang out." In fact, I don't really "just" anything. I *do*.

I'm one of those annoying people who only needs six hours of sleep, which seem to grant me a limitless supply of energy to accomplish lots of things. I derive an unusual amount of joy from checking off my to-do lists. I love to plan and strategize. I even plan when I'm going to plan and strategize, meaning that my plans have plans! Is all of this neurotic? Probably. Does it make me effective at doing? Certainly.

Before planting the church I now pastor, Hope and I went through an assessment process, involving an extensive battery of personality tests, psychometrics, and sit-downs with professional counselors. My results were all so skewed toward activity, achievement, and militant accomplishment that our counselors laughed—literally, out loud—at me.

Then they stopped laughing, and they commiserated with my poor wife.

I don't do rest. I do *do*.

So how in the world does a doer like me get a gig writing a book on rest? Here's the first reason: because if I can learn to stop, so can you.

And if I need to learn to stop, then so do you.

DOING TO DEATH

That brings me to the second reason this project generated a laugh from my wife—a much more serious one. Amid all my doing and achieving, I almost achieved an unexpected outcome: my own demise.

A few years ago, I was in the process of working myself into sickness. The church I pastor was growing fast; we had just moved into the mother of all fixer-uppers, which I was remodeling in the evenings; we had a baby that refused to sleep; we had three other kids who we were attempting to raise (or at least keep alive); we had a marriage we were trying to hold together...

And my world was falling apart.

On the outside, everything looked successful—great job, great wife, great kids, great house—and yet all of this was breaking me. Physically, I was exhausted. Spiritually, I was dry. Emotionally, I was slipping into the deepest depression of my life.

Busy.

Tired.

Anxious.

Yet, I couldn't stop. Of course I couldn't. I live in Boston, and like virtually every other Western city, non-stop work is a virtue here. Busy is compulsory. Pausing is a missed opportunity. If you're busy, you're important. If you're important, you can feel good about yourself. But at some point we get so busy that it stops feeling good.

That's what happened to me. And it almost killed me.

Now, I know what some of you are thinking. "Oh, Adam," you say, "this is simply a time-management problem. If you were a better steward of your time, this wouldn't have happened."

You can say that, but I'll say this: I'll go toe-to-toe with you, calendar to calendar. Because my calendar lays out my slots for my meals, my bedtime, my time with God, even my shower, breakfast, and a workout in the morning. Suffice it to say, I did manage my time well. Just not wisely.

So the second reason I'm writing this book is because not resting almost broke me. After a few months of 70-hour work-weeks, sleepless nights with the most sleep-resistant child we (or possibly anyone else) have yet produced, remodeling a house by myself, and launching a new church, I broke. I never actually knew that I had an end to my will to achieve. But then I achieved that, too. Depression hit hard, my faith was shaken, and—mercifully—God taught me how to rest.

So, I'm writing this book hoping you can learn to rest—how to rest and why you should and why it's great. And I'm hoping that you can start enjoying it before you reach the point of crashing like I did.

I'm writing to introduce you to—or reacquaint you with—Sabbath rest. I'm writing to sell Sabbath rest to you.

CAN'T STOP, WON'T STOP

"Sabbath rest"—it sounds positively puritanical, doesn't it? Western culture fetishizes the frenzied, rushed life. Adverts fill our screens, featuring professional, handsome up-and-comers wearing the latest trend on their way to that important meeting.

Parents rush their kids to practice to ensure the best shot for little Timmy.

Workers rush to their jobs to climb the ladder.

Mothers rush through the bedtime routine to get that well-earned break.

And if you're a Christian, then of course that just piles on another layer of things to do! You're supposed to do all the other stuff (and do it thoughtfully, intentionally, and prayerfully), and give time to church, and make sure you are witnessing to your neighbors, friends, and co-workers. You try to make time to read the Bible, get up early to pray, or stay up later than you'd like listening to someone who needs you. You try to be a better father, husband, mother, child, friend, co-worker, mentor, mentee...

Hurried and frayed, we're not exactly the picture of heaven.

Little wonder then that when we come to Jesus, we bring along with us our need to be busy and our deep-down fear that rest means we're missing out or getting something wrong. Which is strange, because that is the complete opposite of what Jesus asks us to do:

> *Come to me, all who labor and are heavy laden, and I will give you rest. (Matthew 11 v 28)*

When we come to Jesus, we come to the One who accomplished more than any of us ever will, and did so with more restfulness and peace than any of us ever experience. And we come to the One who says that what characterizes a life with him is a lightening of the load and an enjoyment of rest.

So, why can't we stop? Why *won't* we stop?

I think there are two reasons, which will keep cropping up as we go through this book. First, we don't want to believe that we truly need rest; and second, we wish to outdo the other doers. We feel as though we don't have the time even to discuss rest, much less to regularly practice the art—which is exactly why we need to. (And why you score a point for picking up a book on this subject, which should please my fellow achievers no end.)

Oh, and it's because we don't really grasp what rest is. We see it as rules, when in fact rest is art.

REST IS A GIFT AND REST IS AN ART

Some of you are probably thinking as you read this, "The thing is, Adam, all you need to do is observe the Sabbath—stop working on Sunday. You've not done that very well. That's why you had problems." And, while there is something to that critique, there is much more to the art of Sabbath rest than the mere mechanics of a day off.

Then others of you are perhaps from a religious background where "the Sabbath day" was a big deal and strictly observed, and you've moved away from that. The idea of practicing regular rhythms of rest maybe sounds a bit too old-school, a bit formulaic, to you. Restrictions on cooking, chores, and work start to populate your imagination, and before you know it, you're excusing yourself from the whole enterprise— because if that's what rest is, it sounds positively draining, like the kind of thing that leaves you needing a day off, not experiencing one.

Still others of you would love to rest—if only you knew what it was. You wearily wish life felt restful, yet when you stop you feel guilty or lazy, and you worry that you're not doing the stopping right. You suspect that you'd love godly rest—if only you knew how to do it.

We need to learn the art of rest.

We need to learn to hit pause.

As we'll see, biblical rest is less rule and more rhythm—less curmudgeonly restriction and more liberating art form. It is something to be embraced and enjoyed.

Imagine, for a moment, that we're both great musicians. If I play a Bach sonata or shred a Hendrix guitar solo, and then you come along and play said sonata or guitar solo, they will sound different. Assume for a moment that we're both virtuosos, playing with supreme technical accuracy. The music will still sound different. Wonderful, but different.

I think rest is like that.

God has wired us to require rest. Yet when we try to make restrictions and regimens for our restfulness, they seem to miss the mark—like playing the sonata but missing a good handful of notes. But when we see how the story of Jesus frees us to rest and transforms how we see our rest, we get to play the song more beautifully. We don't play because we're being told to (like maybe you used to practice an instrument when you were young, with your mom or your dad standing over you with a stopwatch). We play because we love to.

True rest is a gift given to us in Christ. He is, as the writer of the book of Hebrews says, the hoped-for Sabbath rest for God's people (Hebrews 4 v 9-10), inviting all of us burnt-out achievers, weary parents, worn-down workers, and strung-out students, to come to him and receive rest. Just like music is the gift of the composer to the player, rest is the gift of Jesus to the Christian. And, just like music must be played, rest must be practiced.

Rest is a gift. And rest is an art.

OUR WAY FORWARD

This book is my attempt to offer you a mercifully short starter in the art of rest. Because rest is a sizable theme in the Scriptures, we will journey through both Old and New Testaments to follow the contours of this theme. And because Jesus is the hero of the grand story of Scripture, he'll be the one to whom the whole practice points—the virtuoso in whom rest is embodied and with whom rest is truly enjoyed.

As you read, please remember that you're not listening to a rest expert. I'm not a sweet, gentle, older man who peacefully abides in a tumbledown ranch outside a wispy, quiet village, relaxed and refreshed and rested. No—I'm a rest failure: a natural doer who struggles to relax unless it's timetabled and synced with my calendar app. I'm a consummate achiever in a city of achievers.

But I've started to play the music. I've begun to learn the art of rest. I still miss notes, but I'm getting there. And I'd like to share the tune with you.

We'll start our rehearsal by looking at what rest actually is. With feet firmly rooted in the scriptural story, we'll then discover why rest is so important, and what it means for our relationships. Then, we'll wrap up with a few words on how to actually practice the art of rest. And after that? Well, after that you're on your own.

Not exactly on your own, though. The God of rest is here with me as I write and with you as you read, and is waiting for you in your rest. This is his good gift to us; so let's learn to practice the art of rest.

1. A BIT OF ART HISTORY

"I did overtime, working is such a bind,
Got some money to spend,
Living for the weekend.
When it gets too much, I live for the rush,
Got some money to spend,
Living for the weekend!
Yeah, I've been working all week and I'm shot,
Yeah, I've been working all week, for what?
Just living for the weekend."
Living for the Weekend, by Hard-Fi

I f rest is an art, this chapter is art history.

I know, I know… You want me to tell you exactly how to take a break. "Just give me the goods!"

I get that, because I'm like that. But if we don't take a moment to understand why we rest, then we won't be any better when we rest. After all, if you're anything like me, you need convincing to even take a rest as a regular part of your life, rather than an optional extra after everything else gets done (which it never does.) So we need to learn to want to rest before we get to how to rest. Therefore this chapter will admittedly be the least practical, but possibly the most important. Why?

Because rest is different than you probably think, and more important than you've probably imagined.

WHAT IS REST EXACTLY?

If you speak to my neighbors about rest, they'll probably think you mean a vacation, long nap, or time to binge-watch their favorite show. If you're feeling daring and use the word "Sabbath," you'll likely get weird looks (at least you will in my neighborhood.) But if we let the Bible speak to us about rest, we'll see that it's much more than a day off, and much different than that quirky caricature we may have of Sabbath. Rest is different than you probably think.

Very simply, Sabbath is *a time of rest, holy to the Lord*. It is time that is given to God, to receive refreshment from God.

Cue all the questions! "What day?" "How much time?" "Do we have to call it Sabbath?" "What can I do with that time?" I'd like to ask you to suspend such questions for just a moment (well, a few chapters) so that we can consider what this fascinating and liberating concept is, and where it gets its start in Scripture. So for now, hang on to that simple definition—*Sabbath is a time of rest, holy to the Lord.*

IN THE BEGINNING, REST

Have you ever thought about what God was doing before he did anything? Prior to God bringing time, matter, angels, and everything else into being, the only being was God. Was he hurried, rash, or anxious? Or bored? Or stressed out about the ensuing creation task that lay ahead of him?

Jesus actually tells us the answer. He says to his Father, "You loved me before the foundation of the world" (John 17 v 24). Love. Fullness. Joy. Unhurried satisfaction in the Son was perpetually pouring forth from the Father, from forever past. Prior to spinning out supernovae and cells, God the Father was loving the Son, and the Spirit. And God the Son was loving the Father and the Spirit. And God the Spirit was loving the Father and the Son.

I start here because whatever we think about rest (or anything else), we do so downstream from what we think about God. As the 20th-century pastor A.W. Tozer put it, "What comes into our minds when we think about God is the most important thing about us." If God is a hurried taskmaster constantly turning knobs and pushing buttons, frenetically refining his work, it's hard to imagine resting with him. But if God the Father, Son, and Spirit are the very definition of love, and fundamentally relational, then the idea of resting with him becomes more than imaginable. It becomes desirable.

With lyrical poetry, the first two chapters of Genesis present the reader with God's verdict on his work: good. So good, in fact, that God, pleased with what he made, rested. He did not rest because of tiredness but because of triumph, as someone well pleased with everything that he had done:

> *Thus the heavens and the earth were finished, and all the host of them. And on the seventh day God finished his work that he had done, and he rested on the seventh day from all his work that he had done. So God blessed the seventh day and made it holy, because on it God rested from all his work that he had done in creation.*
> *(Genesis 2 v 1-3)*

God rested.

God didn't rest because he was exhausted, but because he was exhilarated. He had worked hard to make the world; now he was laying down the work to enjoy the world. This was the first Sabbath in the universe. The exhalation of the effort was followed with the inhalation of enjoyment, fulfillment, and satisfaction within the relationships of the Trinity.

You and I are made in the image of this God (Genesis 1 v 26-27). So part of what it means to be human is to rest like God, and rest with God. Our Sabbaths are times of rest with this loving, relational God because the first Sabbath was.

THE TEMPLE OF TIME

The Garden of Eden, where God created humanity to live and work and—yes—rest, was more than God's interesting botanical garden. It was the first true temple—a place where humans dwelt with God perfectly. That's part of what God was doing on that first Sabbath—he rested to dwell in the temple he made, with the people he had made. He had built it, and now it was time to enjoy it with his creatures.

Of course, you know how long that lasted. By chapter 3 of the first book of the Bible, humans had ruined everything and had been evicted from the garden-temple, destined to traverse a world broken by sin.

Yet as the story unfolds and God promises to return his people to the temple of his presence, God's people regularly build altars, beginning to recover what was lost in Eden. Later, God's people would build a tabernacle—a gigantic mobile temple—followed by the actual temple in Jerusalem. Everything about this temple (both the mobile one and the permanent one) was intended to remind the visitor of Eden. Its furnishings, its embroidery, the direction it faced... all of it was Edenic. And when did temple worship take place? On the Sabbath. The place of worship and the time for worship were fused. Temple was the place, and Sabbath the time.

When God made the world, he made space and time. The temple was the space in which God would be with his people, and the Sabbath was the time. That's why God created the Sabbath, to give his people time to be with him, specifically.

God is everywhere, and yet God was present in his temple in a particular, special way. It was the space set apart for his people to come to him.

God was with his people all the time, and yet God was present on his Sabbath in a particular, and particularly special, way. It was the time set apart for his people to be with him.

Today, Christians don't have a temple because after Pentecost we actually became the temple. That is, all those amazing promises that God made all throughout the Scriptures to one day dwell with his people (Exodus 29 v 45; Jeremiah 24 v 7; 31 v 33) have come true. Paul asks the Corinthian church, "Do you not know that you are God's temple and that God's Spirit dwells in you?" (1 Corinthians 3 v 16). We are the temple. But do we have the time—do we *make* the time—to Sabbath, to experience a time holy to God?

That's what Sabbath is. It's the time-temple.

Rest looks different than you probably thought, and more important than you probably imagined.

REST AND ITS ENEMIES

If I were Satan, and had as a big goal in life to make sure Christians were as useless as could be, I would set about trying to convince them of all sorts of great-sounding reasons to rarely, and hopefully, never, get to the time-temple. Let's take a moment to review some of his best work.

1. "I Am What I Do." (The False Virtue of Busyness)
Perhaps the most ingenious lie that the modern world has believed is that to be busy is to be better. We have a strange cultural addiction to busyness. In the West, we've managed to take something that has in every culture until recently been a vice and, through the magic of repeating a bad idea for long enough, have turned it into a virtue! "Oh, I'm so busy this week," we say. But what we're often really saying is, "Look how important I am. I have many things to do, and I must do them."

Some of us even have the audacity to complain to God about our schedules, using busyness as an excuse for not obeying him. That's hilarious, when you pause to think about it. God literally made all things and is currently upholding the universe by his powerful word—he is managing the control panel of history, hearing all pleas, fielding a whole lot of complaints, and keeping track of the ever-decreasing numbers of hairs on our heads, their shortage caused by anxiety from busyness.

And we complain to him that *we're* busy?!

People often try to remind me of how busy I am: "Well, I would have called you and asked for help, Pastor, but I know you're so busy."

I usually smile and tell them, "I'm no busier than you are."

They look at me perplexed, as if I've just rebuffed a compliment. But it's not a compliment. It's complicity with sin.

Every time I hear someone tell me how busy I am, I'm tempted to think, "Well, yes, look at all I do and how important I am." Those words appeal to something in me—and that something is not good, because it's pride. Of course I'm busy, because I'm a human with a job. But busyness is not a virtue. In fact, it could become a vice used by Satan to keep me from God in exchange for a world of jobs that will, if I let them, simply consume my life. The very people who are saved by resting in the grace of the Savior whose final words before his death in our place were "It is finished" have sought to add to those words, "but not quite yet..."

Sabbath rest is the time to be, without being busy. Saying, "I'm too busy to rest" is a bit like saying, "I need too much oxygen to exhale." It just doesn't make sense.

2. *"God's Given Me Too Much to Do!" (The Religious Achiever Reflex)*
Some of you are reading this book about rest because you know you need it. Yet you now feel burdened by me telling you to rest—because you know you can't.

"Fitting in one more thing for God," you say, "is just not going to work."

You're busy with the kids, with work, with school, with church—with obeying God in all of life. How can God expect you to take a day off when you're already working so hard to do all the other things he's asked of you? It's like Pharaoh forcing the Israelites to make bricks with fewer materials at the same pace (Exodus 5 v 1-21).

But chances are, you're hiding. In Peter Scazzero's book, *Emotionally Healthy Spirituality*, there's a great list of ways you can know if you have an emotionally unhealthy spirituality. One of those signs is using God to hide from God. You use God's instructions about parenting, productivity, and giving your life away to Christian service to hide from God himself—from ever being with him and relating to him.

At its worst, good-stuff-for-God puts us in charge and lets us feel like we have deserved blessing. Or it lets us hide from the fact that we are not sure we even know the real God. If we can't stop, that suggests that this is the case.

Rest is not a religious action item to be added to a list. It isn't a duty to be performed; it's a delight to be enjoyed. If you can't rest because you're busy doing all these things for God, then pick some of the ones that are optional and stop doing them so that you can obey his non-optional command and invitation to rest with him. God's enemy wants nothing more than to use this lie to torpedo your relationship with God, one "good" activity at a time.

3. *"If I Stop, Life Just Won't Work Out." (The Irreligious False Heaven)*

There are a thousand ways to reach "heaven."

Working too hard? Just work even harder so you can get to the restful heaven of retirement.

Stressed out by your kids? Just stress out a little more in your helicopter parenting so you can get to the heaven of perfect children.

Feeling lonely? Spend thousands of hours at the gym becoming that well-shaped sexual conqueror so you can get to the heaven of frequent pleasure.

So many books, seminars, and techniques are designed to help you get the things in this world that seem they'll bring you that restful paradise you're longing for.

Of course, none of those heavens exist.

Retired people don't retire from life. They often find upon entering retirement that the only change is that they now no longer have their jobs to cover over the deep pain and dysfunction in their souls. There's no rest there.

Perfect children don't exist either. They can't be created by parents who lose sleep worrying where to find organic, locally-sourced, fairly-traded notebook paper for little Johnny's Montessori school assignments. There's no rest there.

Sexual heaven doesn't exist either. You can exercise all you want, eat the best food, get all the plastic surgery, and have all the sex you can manage. But you'll find that the body of your dreams will still age, get sick, turn wrinkly, and eventually die. There's no rest there.

Here's the truth: in order to reach them, all of these false Sabbaths require you to work harder with no rest. Yet, when you finally get them—the money, the family, the body—they don't bring the rest they promised. They lied.

I grew up around really rich, really successful people. One man, with more money than he knew what to do with, appeared to enjoy it. There was often a new girl on his arm, and regularly a new car outside his house. But, before long, his long years of pursuing a false, irreligious heaven caught up with him, and his dream faded. He died a sick, lonely man. His funeral was hopelessly sad.

All these things—work, money, kids, health, sex, food, and drink—are good. God made each of them. But pursued too much, for the wrong reasons, they don't bring us rest. They burn us out.

True rest is different than you may have thought. And I hope you can see that finding it is more important than you may have imagined.

REST IS ABOUT WHO RULES

I have a vivid memory of the first time my restlessness expressed itself. It was in preparation for a high school musical. I was directing the orchestra. A gigantic music nerd, I carefully studied the score, selected the musicians, and ran the rehearsals. Yet on one rehearsal day, I was sick and I couldn't make it. This filled me with anxiety, which wasn't helped when a friend of mine called as I lay in bed, offering to lead it. My reply betrayed my arrogance:

"No! If I don't do it, it won't be done right!"

Even if you aren't as neurotic as I was in my teen years, you probably have a hard time stopping—even when in sickness your body is begging you to take a break—because life needs you to be doing, so that it gets done right.

No.

The first time we encounter the command to Sabbath, it reads like this:

> [8] *Remember the Sabbath day, to keep it holy. [9] Six days you shall labor, and do all your work, [10] but the seventh day is a Sabbath to the LORD your God. On it you shall not do any work, you, or your son, or your daughter, your male servant, or your female servant, or your livestock, or the sojourner who is within your gates.* [11] *For in six days the LORD made heaven and earth, the sea, and all that is in them, and rested on the seventh day. Therefore the LORD blessed the Sabbath day and made it holy. (Exodus 20 v 8-11)*

In verse 11, the word "for" starts the explanatory clause for the command to rest. And what does it say?

Stop, because God made everything.

In our refusal to rest, what we're doing is far worse than merely not taking care of ourselves. We're actually telling a different story than what we say we believe. We're quite happy to sing and study about the God who rules. We just don't believe what we say enough to regularly lay down our rule. We creatures, made to co-create with God, have so idolized our creative work that we refuse to honor God as the Creator. Yet that's exactly what Sabbath rest is about.

It is a declaration to ourselves, our kids, our communities, and even our demanding bosses that we don't worship work or its results.

It is a declaration that our work is not sufficient for our lives to thrive or necessary for this world to thrive.

Regular rest is the practice by which we say with our lives, "The God who made the world rules the world, and I trust him to do it better than me."

Resting requires you to admit that you are not sufficient, and to acknowledge that there is One who is. You are not a sufficient explanation of your own life, nor are you enough in yourself to find true and lasting Sabbath rest in this life. Embracing a rhythm of rest means seeing God as sufficient and letting go of your own claim to that attribute.

We worship God. God made the work, God made the world, and so God made us to rest.

REST IS ABOUT WHO RESCUES

In the final book of the Torah, the first five books of the Old Testament, the command to rest was restated slightly differently:

> [12] *Observe the Sabbath day, to keep it holy, as the* LORD *your God commanded you.* [13] *Six days you shall labor and do all your work,* [14] *but the seventh day is a Sabbath to the* LORD *your God. On it you shall not do any work, you or your son or your daughter or your male servant or your female servant, or your ox or your donkey or any of your livestock, or the sojourner who is within your gates, that your male servant and your female servant may rest as well as you.* [15] *You shall remember that you were a slave in the land of Egypt, and the* LORD *your God brought you out from there with a mighty hand and an outstretched arm. Therefore the* LORD *your God commanded you to keep the Sabbath day.*
>
> *(Deuteronomy 5 v 12-15)*

Everything about this passage sounds pretty much like the original, except for verse 15. Instead of commanding the Israelites to rest because resting declares that he rules, they are commanded to rest because he is their rescuer. When God delivered the people of Israel from Pharaoh, the false god-king of Egypt, he was declaring, for the whole world to see, who was the real rescuer.

Slavish devotion to work and the world is subhuman, and in the exodus, God demonstrated that he and he alone saves us from that slavery.

Jesus, the greater Moses whom Moses himself promised would come (Deuteronomy 18 v 15), offers us an even better exodus story. As bad as Pharaoh was, he was small potatoes compared to Satan. That old serpent has wrought more ruin in God's world than any king or despot ever could. And Jesus has freed us from him.

Embracing Jesus as my Savior means admitting that I need saving from systems that demand I keep working and achieving. And it means accepting that I need saving from my own heart, which signs up so willingly to those systems because I want it to be about me, and what I do. But where the world demands that I never stop doing, the gospel declares that it's all been done. I don't rescue myself. And that's okay, because I've already been rescued.

But God has given you so much to do, and if you stop you won't get it done, right? And no one can do what you do like you can do it, right? When you begin to feel these lies anxiously crawling into your ears, hear the gospel remind you that you're not essential, that your work could never build eternity—and that that is fine, because it doesn't need to. God already did it all, in Jesus:

> [8] *By grace you have been saved through faith. And this is not your own doing; it is the gift of God,* [9] *not a result of works. (Ephesians 2 v 8-9)*

You won't lose anything by resting that you need to keep, and you won't gain anything by overwork that you won't one day lose. He is the rescuer.

REST IS ABOUT REGAINING AND REFRESHING

"You were not pleasant to be around tonight," she said.

I was a little miffed upon hearing these words. But actually, I'd been a little miffed all day. My wife was cleaning up after dinner, I had just put the kids to bed, and she needed to confront me.

"You act like the kids and I are getting in your way. Like we're a burden to you. You were short-tempered with them at dinner, unkind to me, and you need to know that it's not okay."

I didn't have much to say, because I knew she was right. I apologized and the conversation turned more fruitful, but it took me a few days to reflect on why, exactly, this happens. Why do I become so short-fused with my family, but have more grace with my church? Why does my daughter needing help with homework bother me more than a staff member calling me for help with their work? Then it dawned on me. I was getting my refreshment from my work, and it was turning me against my family.

Work is a great gift. But in my work-worship, I had begun to feed emotionally from the wrong place. I preferred to hear, "Pastor Adam, great sermon today," than to spend time with my family. It had finally gotten to such a state that even on my days of rest with my family, I didn't want to be with them. I'd taken the gift of work and made it the god I served; and I was happy to declare emotional holy war on anyone who got in my way.

Sabbath rest is about regaining our emotional and physical capital from God. It is the act of stopping long enough to breathe in his refreshing power. When Jesus cried out, "Come to me, all who labor and are heavy laden, and I will give you rest" (Matthew 11 v 28), he actually meant what he said. Sabbath rest enables me to remember that I can actually regain the emotional and physical energy that I need to serve Jesus, from Jesus.

He is not a stingy slave-driver, like Pharaoh was.

He is not demanding that I make bricks from straw.

He is the abundant grace-giver.

I need to stop long enough to repent of my over-love for work, remember that I'm made for him, and practice the art of resting in him to receive actual, real, tangible refreshing for every part of my life.

FIGHT FALSE REST, FIND GOD'S GRACE

The refusal to stop is a refusal to accept our creatureliness. It is a subtle rejection of God's ability to rule his world, rescue his people, and rejuvenate them along the way. Rest—a time holy to the Lord—declares who rules, who rescues, and who refreshes. True Sabbath rest is about learning a new rhythm to life where we celebrate the sovereignty of God, enjoy the liberation of the gospel, and truly trust the salvation Jesus gives. That's why Psalm 127 v 2 says:

It is in vain that you rise up early and go late to rest, eating the bread of anxious toil; for he gives to his beloved sleep.

So rest probably looks different now than it did at the beginning of the chapter; and hopefully, you're starting to see how it's also much more important. So important that it's worth fighting for it.

So, stop.

Embrace the idea that God has called you to rest—to set apart regular time for him to refresh you. A time that is unhurried, but pregnant with meaning; that is unpressured, but about who is ultimately in charge. Sabbath rest may look different that you had thought; and it's almost certainly far more important than you have imagined.

2. REST ALLOWS REMEMBERING

"Remembering becomes a tool that sees us through present pain and difficulties and propels us into new, faith-filled spaces, preparing us for the future."
Stones of Remembrance, by Lois Evans

It was the strangest and most wonderful Thanksgiving dinner I can remember.

When Hope and I were first together, like most couples, we told each other all about ourselves. She told me where she was from. She told me about life growing up in rural northern Louisiana—the maid, her father's old wooden TV that looked like a piece of furniture, the fruit trees in the backyard, and her earliest memories in the house.

I knew all that.

But the first time I accompanied her back to her family home for Thanksgiving, I suddenly, viscerally, *knew* it.

When we entered the home, the sights, smells, and people suddenly brought to life all the things she had told me. Eating there with her family caused me to remember all kinds of things I'd known about the woman I loved, but had forgotten—or, perhaps, never fully grasped. The turkey, the pumpkin pie, and the noise of the football game coming through that dusty old television did something to me. The way the little tastes, sights, and sounds came together helped me know my wife more deeply, as I shared this annual American ritual with the people who raised her.

Rituals are like that. They cause us to remember (or re-remember) deep, personal truths that would otherwise fade to the back our minds. Holiday meals remind us of family. Birthdays remind us of ourselves. National celebrations remind us of our nations and their stories.

And the ritual of biblical rest reminds us of our God, and his story. Rest is given for us to remember God, ourselves, and the true story of the world.

THE COST OF FORGETFULNESS

God's people had suffered from a kind spiritual amnesia ever since their inception. With stunning regularity they forgot who they were, whose they were, and for what purpose God had called them in the first place. The story of the whole Bible is in many ways the story of a people who always forget their God, and a God who always remembers his people.

The first members of God's people—Abraham, Isaac, and Jacob—struggled to keep their eye on the ball, and so they sinned inexcusably and struggled when they didn't have to.

Their children and grandchildren were no better. By little more than a generation after Moses, the book of Judges chronicles the downward spiral of our spiritual forebears—people who failed to keep the practices of memory. Reading the book of Judges isn't like thumbing through a scrapbook of Bible heroes. It's like shuffling through the rap sheets of failures, fools, and a whole mess of distracted, once-delivered people who "forgot the LORD their God and served the Baals and the Asheroth," the false gods of the surrounding culture (Judges 3 v 7). The whole book of Judges is a warning of the horrendous results of spiritual forgetfulness.

After the judges, we get kings. They started fairly well, but three generations after the great King David, the second king of Israel, the kingdom was fractured. The people, forgetting who they were, became virtually indistinguishable from everyone else. After giving them plenty of warnings through his prophets, the Lord caused them to live with everyone else, as foreign nations came and invaded Israel.

This invasion culminated in the final destruction of the temple, the exile of the Jews, and a time of wandering obscurity for the people of God. Over and over again,

God's people forgot who they were, whose they were, and the reason they were there in the first place.

As they sat in exile, the questions everyone must have been asking were, "Why?" and "What exactly went wrong?" The prophet Ezekiel was given some insight into this understandable question. God gave him a message to a people who had almost entirely lost the plot. Here is God's answer to the "Why?" question:

> [12] *I gave them my Sabbaths, as a sign between me and them, that they might know that I am the LORD who sanctifies them.* [13] *But the house of Israel rebelled against me in the wilderness. They did not walk in my statutes but rejected my rules, by which, if a person does them, he shall live; and my Sabbaths they greatly profaned.*
>
> *Then I said I would pour out my wrath upon them in the wilderness, to make a full end of them.* [14] *But I acted for the sake of my name, that it should not be profaned in the sight of the nations, in whose sight I had brought them out.* [15] *Moreover, I swore to them in the wilderness that I would not bring them into the land that I had given them, a land flowing with milk and honey, the most glorious of all lands,* [16] *because they rejected my rules and did not walk in my statutes, and profaned my Sabbaths; for their heart went after their idols.* [17] *Nevertheless, my eye spared them, and I did not destroy them or make a full end of them in the wilderness.*

¹⁸ "And I said to their children in the wilderness, "Do not walk in the statutes of your fathers, nor keep their rules, nor defile yourselves with their idols. ¹⁹ I am the LORD your God; walk in my statutes, and be careful to obey my rules, ²⁰ and keep my Sabbaths holy that they may be a sign between me and you, that you may know that I am the Lord your God." ²¹ But the children rebelled against me. They did not walk in my statutes and were not careful to obey my rules, by which, if a person does them, he shall live; they profaned my Sabbaths. (Ezekiel 20 v 12-21)

Do you hear the tragedy in Ezekiel's words? God's people hadn't shown up for their Thanksgiving Dinner. "I gave them my Sabbaths ... and my Sabbaths they greatly profaned." They skipped Sabbath rest, and as they let go of the ritual of rest, they forgot what they most needed to remember, and let go of all that they most needed to grasp. They let go of God. Curses, pain, and exile ensued.

AN ANATOMY OF SPIRITUAL AMNESIA

I can relate to exiled Israel. Maybe you can, too. It's so easy to let go of the rhythm of rest, forget all that rest is meant to help us remember, let loose a flood of issues, and by that stage be so far into forgetfulness that we wonder where all these issues came from and how on earth we might turn the tide.

The physical issues are first. Then come the emotional ones. Finally, the spiritual weakness and passionlessness arrive. Perhaps for you it started with a life transition: a new baby, a job loss, the workload of school, or climbing the career ladder. It was only going to be once... or for a season... but you stopped showing up for the Sabbath rest, for the Christian Thanksgiving dinner.

Maybe the first time it was an accident.

The second time it was expedient.

And now... well, now you can't remember why you ever rested in the first place. You're caught in a new ritual— one without rest.

How does this happen? What leads to this spiritual amnesia?

It's irritatingly simple: we forget when we forget to remember.

God gave Israel the Sabbath—the special day of rest, remembrance, recuperation, and recreation. Life in the ancient Near East was hard—harder, I dare say, than most of our lives. Working for food from sunrise to sunset, living off the land, in constant danger of being attacked by neighboring tribes—that was their life. The idea of taking a day away from toil must have seemed a little crazy. And yet it was this day that was given to them as their ritual, so that they could remember.

But they didn't keep the ritual. They dismissed the art of rest. They forgot to remember.

Maybe they forgot to remember why they needed to rest:

"Was it for rest? Or worship? Or... well, never mind. It's a busy season of the year and it's almost time for harvest. Better put in a few more hours of work..."

When we forget the reason for the ritual of rest, it becomes pretty easy to forget the rest itself.

In our family, every Thursday night is family movie night. We began this ritual back when our first child was barely able to watch a movie, but the idea wasn't the movie itself. It was to build a family moment into the week—an intentional time of togetherness.

But, over the years, the night started to change.

Gradually, Hope and I found this a good moment to get a little extra work done, or to take a moment for ourselves, while the kids were sitting still and quiet. Then, it got less quiet as the kids began to argue over the movie, or the popcorn, or whatever. Over a period of time, we allowed ourselves to forget the point of the ritual, and so it stopped working. In fact, because we forgot the reason for the ritual, we had already started forging new rituals (like work, extra time out, and so on).

Israel had done the same thing. First, they forgot the reasons for the ritual. Then they forged new rituals, until finally they forgot the godly rituals altogether. And with that, they forgot to remember the great truths that the ritual was intended to remind them of. It's no different for us when it comes to Christian rest. The Sabbath ritual of rest is given for us to remember God, ourselves, and the true story of the world. Letting go of rest means acquiescing to the spiritual amnesia that so tragically marked our forebears.

REST IS TO REMEMBER GOD

Kids have activities. I have work. School needs doing. The house needs fixing. The dog needs walking. On top of that, the poor need help, the gospel needs to be preached, and the nations need to be reached. How can we do all God has called us to do if we're stopping every week!?

> *I gave them my Sabbaths, as a sign between me and them, that they might know that I am the LORD...*

Forgetting rest means forgetting God.

I fully understand that we are not under the same obligations as ancient Israel. I realize that, as Christians, Sabbath obedience is not identically incumbent upon us as it was for God's Old Testament people (and yes, we'll talk about that later on—but not yet.) But, while it is not identical, it is certainly analogical. If you're concerned that by embracing regular Sabbath rest you're in danger of coming under some harsh legalism, simply ask yourself how *not* observing Sabbath rest is going for you. It's not rest that threatens to oppress you, but your refusal to. If living restlessly is going great, and you're thriving in your Christian life while never enjoying a time holy to the Lord, you should probably put this book down and call a publisher, so you can write a best-selling rebuttal of the book you hold in your hands.

But if you reflect for a moment, you'll probably realize that the non-stop pace of Western-world life is neither physically sustainable nor spiritually beneficial. It is, however, a remarkably effective way to slowly forget God. And that's just the point. God gave us regular, weekly times to stop in order to know (because we're bound to forget) that it is God who is God, not us.

REST IS TO REMEMBER US

Constant work turns human beings into human doings.

The gods of the ancient Near East never allowed their followers to stop. With a ceaseless appetite for war, worship, wealth, and work, these pagan deities wore out their followers and never delivered on their promises. When the prophets of Baal took on Elijah, the prophet of the LORD, in the great "Who can prove their god is real?" contest on Mount Carmel, they worked hard:

> [26] They ... called upon the name of Baal from morning until noon, saying, "O Baal, answer us!" But there was no voice, and no one answered. And they limped around the altar that they had made. [27] And at noon Elijah mocked them, saying, "Cry aloud, for he is a god. Either he is musing, or he is relieving himself, or he is on a journey, or perhaps he is asleep and must be awakened." [28] And they cried aloud and cut themselves after their

custom with swords and lances, until the blood gushed out upon them. [29] *And as midday passed, they raved on until the time of the offering of the oblation, but there was no voice. No one answered; no one paid attention.*

(1 Kings 18 v 26-29)

We're incredibly similar. As good, modern people, we scoff at the idea of Baal worship or Asheroth prayers. Yet we sing songs about sex, money, and power. We study and strive to move up the ladder, and get the home and the car. We fastidiously watch what we eat out of concern for the shape of our body, for health, and for safety. We're no better than the prophets of Baal, flogging ourselves just to get our false god to pay us back for our efforts. We're just like them.

This is not who we're meant to be.

The God of the Bible is different. He demands no work before he will bless those who love him and live for him:

[36] *Elijah the prophet came near and said, "O LORD, God of Abraham, Isaac, and Israel, let it be known this day that you are God in Israel, and that I am your servant, and that I have done all these things at your word.* [37] *Answer me, O LORD, answer me, that this people may know that you, O LORD, are God, and that you have turned their hearts back."* [38] *Then the fire of the LORD fell and consumed the burnt offering [of a bull] and the wood and the stones and the dust, and licked up the water that was in the trench. (1 Kings 18 v 36-38)*

Unlike the prophets of Baal—who were citizens of Israel and should have known better—Elijah remembered who God is. He did not work till he dropped. He prayed.

Which approach to life better describes you?

They did not walk in my statutes but rejected my rules, by which, if a person does them, he shall live; and my Sabbaths they greatly profaned...

Rejecting regular rest means we reject right living. We are little image-bearers of a great God. We are sons and daughters of the true King. Regular rest is when we turn back to him whose image we're meant to reflect. It's given for us to remember:

"Oh yeah, my money is not who I am. I'm not just a tool for productivity. My value lies not in what I do but in who I am. My identity is in being an image-bearer, not in my contribution to the economy or my status in my community. I'm a human, made for God, by God, to be with God."

REST IS TO REMEMBER THE MEANING OF LIFE

There is an insidious and popular false gospel that threatens to steal your faith in God, obliterate your joy, and destroy your purpose. It's the false gospel of expressive individualism.

This "gospel" tells its adherents that the true problem with the world isn't that our selfward turn has disrupted our relationship with God, but that religion threatens to oppress you by preventing you from expressing yourself. This story says that, instead of needing to be restored to your Creator by freely accepting his grace, you need to be liberated from all authority so you can finally self-actualize your authentic self. We don't need to place ourselves under God's loving words and wisdom, but to look inward to discover our own words and wisdom.

This bag of bad ideas pervades our social media feeds, our parenting books, our news, our music—pretty much every part of our lives. And if we embrace it, we do so at the cost of letting go of the actual meaning of life. We were not made to make ourselves great. We were made to marvel at God's greatness.

> *... because they rejected my rules and did not walk in my statutes, and profaned my Sabbaths; for their heart went after their idols.*

How do we remember that this is not where we find the meaning of life? We stop. We disengage from the media, the message, the music of the world. This isn't the bogeyman of fundamentalism returning to tell you, *Come ye out from among them!* This is the wisdom of your Father, saying, *Come here so you can be effective among them.*

Regularly stopping to rest in God allows us to remember that the meaning of our lives isn't to wander around inside ourselves and choose what aspect of our desires we'll wear as an identity badge.

For Israel, Sabbath forgetfulness was connected to idol worship. Forgetting the rhythm of rest allowed them to forget the true meaning of life, and meant that there was a life-purpose-shaped gap that had to be filled by something. No longer pausing to marvel at God, their eyes were drawn to the glitter of golden statues. Claiming to be wise, they became fools and exchanged the rhythm of remembering the glory of the immortal God for images that resembled birds and animals (Romans 1 v 22-23).

Paul was right then, and he sure seems right now, too. The only difference is that we don't stop to admire glittering statues of birds and animals. We stare at mirrors. We lift our hands to honor pagan deities as we raise our arms to take perfect selfies. We have forgotten the Creator and replaced him with the creature. We have made the meaning of life to find ourselves, rather than to find God.

This version of spiritual hide-and-seek to which we have condemned ourselves—ever seeking ourselves and ever ignoring God—is utterly futile and doomed to failure, because we will only know ourselves rightly when we know God. Augustine put it brilliantly way back in the sixth century:

"Our hearts are restless until they find their rest in Thee."

Thee. Not *Me.*

REST IS TO REMEMBER GRACE

That counterfeit gospel I mentioned above has a false future hope built in—that as we throw off the shackles of religion, external authority, and tradition, we'll become truly human and truly happy.

And if you don't think about it for too long, that sounds really great, doesn't it? I mean, it sure seems like the world is gradually becoming a better place. Technology, wealth, education, and medicine... these all hold great promise for bringing us into a kind of utopia that previous generations of humans could only dream of. So, as long as we work hard for those things, and work hard to become our truest selves, then we'll make the world a better, brighter place for the generations to come.

This great secular hope is the kingdom into which much of our labor is designed to bring us.

The only problem is that this false story can never, ever deliver on its promises. In fact, it dooms its believers, both if they achieve some approximation of the dream of self-actualization, and if they don't. If you never get to meet your truest self, even after extreme effort, you're bound to feel badly about that. Yet, if you actually do achieve some version of this false dream of heaven, then you'll see with stunning clarity that it is not enough to actually save you or the world. You will still die. The world will still suffer. And no matter what you achieve in this life, it's most likely that a generation or two after you pass, no one will remember you, or the person you thought you truly were.

> *But I acted for the sake of my name, that it should not be profaned in the sight of the nations, in whose sight I had brought them out. Moreover, I swore to them in the wilderness that I would not bring them into the land that I had given them, a land flowing with milk and honey, the most glorious of all lands.*

The practice of regular rest reminds us of the grace of God in the gospel, because it allows us the gift of pausing and reflecting long enough to once again realize that we cannot save the world. We can help, and we should. But our ultimate hope is not in ceaseless striving to save and satisfy ourselves, but in the ceaseless certainty that God has saved us and can truly satisfy.

He brings us out from death.

He sets before us a glorious, eternal land.

Salvation lies in God and what he graciously gives, not in me and what I grasp to gain.

Moreover, God's commitment to us isn't even based on us. God acts "for the sake of [his] name." Just as God promised "the most glorious of all lands" on earth to Israel, so his commitment to bring us into the most glorious land eternally is based on his complete commitment to the glory of his name among the nations.

Pause and reflect on the goodness of that news.

No, really.

Stop.

Rest now. Cease trying to finish a chapter a day right now. Put the book down, and pause, reflect, and revel in this truth.

God loves you, God has saved you, God has in store for you a future so dazzling your mind cannot comprehend it. There is nothing you have done to deserve all that—nothing—and that's OK, because it's all freely given. This is all true of anyone who trusts in Christ. Anyone. You.

Re-read that paragraph.

Rest in it.

Truly reveling in it requires stopping to reflect because we're so serially tempted to forget. God gave us the gift of rest to remember God, ourselves, and the true story of the world.

REST TO REMEMBER

I can't eat Thanksgiving dinner without remembering that first one that I shared with my wife's family. The ritual calls back the memory. And upon recalling it, I remember and am grateful—grateful for her, for our story, and for this moment to be grateful.

We need ritual rest because we need to regularly remember. God knows we need it, and he also knows that the risks in forgetting are legion. Regular rest is our remembering ritual. If we let busyness, distraction, or even good work carry us off too far from it, then we'll forget to remember. And, eventually, we'll replace the ritual of rest with some other ritual—house work, homework, voluntary work, or some other good-sounding stand-in for the Sabbath we actually need.

Recently, Hope and I decided to change the way we do family movie night a bit, in order to renew our commitment to be intentionally together. No more sneaking off to get a bit of work done, taking the opportunity to be alone, or simply catching up on chores. As you approach the art of rest, take a moment to reflect on how God might like to remodel the ritual of Sabbath rest for you, so you can remember who you are, whose you are, and the purpose for which you've been made to be his in the first place.

3. REST IS RESISTANCE

"When I run, I feel his pleasure..."
Eric Liddell, *Chariots of Fire*

"I [have] ten lonely seconds to justify my whole existence."
Harold Abrams, *Chariots of Fire*

The epic movie *Chariots of Fire* chronicles the rise of Eric Liddell to fame at the 1924 Olympics. A passionate man of God, Liddell uttered the famous line, "When I run, I feel his pleasure." For him, the work of running was an offering to God.

But the movie also has a counter-hero, Harold Abrahams. For Abrahams, running isn't about pleasing God—it's about proving his purpose. Running gave him "ten lonely seconds to justify my whole existence."

All your work will be done for one of these two ends: to glorify God or to justify yourself. And if your work is really just your ten lonely seconds—or 70 hours a week—to justify your whole existence, rest will be out of the question. It would be a waste of time, a sign of weakness, or an admission of failure.

But for followers of Jesus, rest isn't a sign of weakness. Rest is an act of profound resistance against the siren call of self-justification. It's not about admitting weakness. It's about having the strength to resist.

WHAT DO YOU DO?

Remember the story of the exodus? God's people were enslaved to Pharaoh, a false god-king who demanded ceaseless work so that he could live in ceaseless pleasure. You're probably glad you don't live under his rule.

Oh, but many of us do.

The god of this world is no better. Satan is a false god-king, and he stands behind the worldview that promotes a false gospel of self-justification. In big, Western metropolises like the one in which I live, the message is very clear: you are what you do.

Don't believe me? Think about the last few times you met someone. What did you say? I'll bet that your top three questions were aimed at finding out their name, their family set-up... and their career. "What do you do?" is a question that comes very fast in a conversation with someone we've just met. And "How's work?" comes equally fast when we speak with someone we know a little better.

Our desire to answer the "What do you do?" question in a way that sounds impressive is what drives students to study, motivates some to work, pushes many to over-work, and causes others to mourn. When we ask it of someone else, the answer we hear shows us where to place this new acquaintance on the mental chart we all carry around with us that lists our relationships in order of importance. You may think that sounds terrible, and it is; but it also sounds like every networking event I've ever attended.

This deeply-embedded attitude is less obvious than Israel's slavery in Egypt, but no less dehumanizing. The world without and our hearts within demand we justify our own existence; and that is a kind of slavery of which Pharaoh's slave drivers could only dream. Why? Because it dooms us to a prison from which we can never escape. We are insufficient to explain our own existence. So we work for the one thing that we're unable to give ourselves: meaning... purpose... a justification for our own existence.

We all walk through our prison with our uniforms on—not stripes, but suits and ties or factory overalls or rubber gloves.

Sabbath rest, however, says that I don't need to justify my own existence. It's an act of resistance against the false god-king of this world who always demands that we do. It's open rebellion against the systems of this world that demand we do in order to be.

RESIST FALSE RULERS

Jesus was an incredibly non-anxious person. If I had been tasked with the salvation of the world, I would have been a bit more uptight. Yet, because Christ was so secure in his relationship with his Father, he was so secure in his work for his Father that he could embrace and explain Sabbath rest rightly—even when he was challenged about it:

> [1] On a Sabbath, while he was going through the grainfields, his disciples plucked and ate some heads of grain, rubbing them in their hands. [2] But some of the Pharisees said, "Why are you doing what is not lawful to do on the Sabbath?" [3] And Jesus answered them, "Have you not read what David did when he was hungry, he and those who were with him: [4] how he entered the house of God and took and ate the bread of the Presence, which is not lawful for any but the priests to eat, and also gave it to those with him?" [5] And he said to them, "The Son of Man is lord of the Sabbath."
>
> (Luke 6 v 1-5)

Contrasting with Jesus' peaceful demeanor are the Pharisees—Jewish religious ninjas. I use that term because at this point in history they had constructed 39 rules around the practice of resting. That's right—these people came up with 39 ways to correctly do nothing. So when they saw that Jesus' disciples were rubbing grain in their hands to release the husk from the fruit on a Sabbath, they panicked.

You're breaking the rules!

You're not resting correctly!

Stop stopping wrong!

It sounds laughable, but this scene wasn't a joke to anyone in it. These men were angry with Jesus because in his act of rest, he was openly defying their power and their position. This is exactly what Jesus meant to do, because he wanted to make something clear—that he, not they, was "lord of the Sabbath." Ironically, the Pharisees sought to obey God's rules for rest without letting him be the Lord of that rest. Rest matters to God. He's in charge of it.

It would be easy for us to simply nod along while Jesus rebukes the Pharisees, because we would never make the mistake of taking Sabbath too seriously. But maybe that's because we don't take rest seriously at all. It's easy to raise our eyebrows at their panic over rubbing some husks while being blind to the fact that we're just as wrong in our Sabbath ignoring as they were in their Sabbath policing.

Notice that in his answer, Jesus neither accepted their version of Sabbath rest, nor did he say that there is no such thing as Sabbath rest. We embrace the art of rest and resist the gospel of self-justification by allowing Jesus to be the Lord of our Sabbath.

RESIST THE ANXIETY

Anxiety is what unbelief feels like.

Therefore, our feelings about rest betray whether we really trust Jesus—with our time, our work, our weeks, and our lives.

I have spent much of my life enduring the feeling of anxiety. Often, we are driven to do because we are trying to dull the tight, churning sense of angst that simmers and boils up when we don't. Contrast this with Jesus. Has anyone accomplished more than him? I mean, I'm writing this book right now, which is taking a good degree of work. He, on the other hand, had before him the simple job of defeating Satan, sin, death, hell, and the grave. And yet no one would read the Gospels and come away with the impression that Jesus was all pent up with that pressure. Why? Because he is the Lord of Sabbath—the ruler of and the great artist of rest.

If anxiety is what unbelief feels like, then restful peace is the inheritance of those who trust Jesus.

When we were born, we came into a world system like Pharaoh's. Work is demanded to explain our existence and earn our rest. But when we were born again into God's new world through Jesus, we were born into a new system. Work is a calling to serve our King who died to give us rest. It is a way that we please him. Work and rest are just ways we enjoy his pleasure. Jesus, as it turns out, is quite a bit better than Pharaoh.

In his little book on Sabbath, Walter Brueggemann wrote:

> *In our own contemporary context of the rat race of anxiety, the celebration of Sabbath is a point of both resistance and alternative. It is resistance because it is a visible insistence that our lives are not defined by the production and consumption of commodity goods ... But Sabbath is not only resistance. It is alternative. It is an alternative to the demanding, chattering, pervasive presence of advertising and the great liturgical claim of professional sports that devour all our "rest time." The alternative on offer is the awareness and practice of the claim that we are situated on the receiving end of the gifts of God. (Sabbath as Resistance, xiv)*

We are situated on the receiving end of the gifts of God, not on the earning end.

The Pharisees were angry with Jesus because their sense of rest and sense of self depended on their obedience to a set of rules neither authored by God nor oriented toward human good. Yet Jesus was at peace because he knew true rest depended on the grace of God, which was for humanity's good. The Pharisees' rules lied to them about Sabbath. Our world's rules lie just as much.

So here's a simple question—whose emotions mirror your own? Rest will produce anxiety in the person who does not rely on Jesus as Lord; but the person who knows Jesus as Lord will rest to resist anxiety. That's the difference.

RESIST AUTONOMY

"Did God really say...?" was the first question offered by Satan in his attempt to undermine God's work in the world (Genesis 3 v 1, NIV). This question is a favorite of the natural-born rebel.

"Did God really say I need a day of rest?"

"Did God really say I need to take time out?"

But the natural-born rule-keepers are often quick to add a word, and it's equally undermining to God's work:

"Did God really say enough?"

Autonomy comes from two Greek words (*autos* and *nomos*) which mean "self-law," and the ruler of this world is quite happy to let you believe that you have autonomy in spades. You don't really, of course. But in thinking you do, you happily wander deeper into his labyrinth.

Good religious folk know that autonomy is wrong, so they try to exit the maze of life through the path of getting God's law just right. But that's no better, because when we add to God's words, we're just doing what we want to do, running our lives in the way that seems best to us. We're sneaking autonomy through the back door of the church.

"Did God really say?" and "Did God really say enough?" are two questions that drive us deeper into sin and exhaustion. They come from two different starting points—the rebellious and the religious—but they both spring from the heart that craves to be autonomous.

Biblical rest, then, is an act of resistance against this two-faced autonomy. It's a practice that says no to the gnawing hunger we have to run our own lives, because it sets up a regular reminder that Jesus is the Lord of our lives.

Think about the language we use. "I've got to be me." "I want to be authentic." "You do you." Or sometimes even the Christian-sounding obsession with "What is God's will for my life?" These are the credal confessions of the First Church of Self-determination, Autonomyville. This church preaches that in order for you to be the most you-ey you you can be, you just need to look within.

Just dive into the deep, dark cave of self and start digging...

Keep going...

And maybe, buried there under the barnacles, you'll find your youiest you to put on display for your fulfillment and for all to love.

Gosh, that's a lot of pressure. It starts off sounding cool in the adolescent dream of teenage angst. But the truth is that you only come into contact with your truest self when you come closer to Christ. You won't find you by clambering about in your own subconscious, but by bringing your whole self to him.

Rest helps you run away from the cave and into the fields to share a meal with your Savior. Eating with Jesus in the fields on the Sabbath wasn't about sticking it to the man (irreligious autonomy) or faithfully following all thirty-nine rules (religious autonomy). It was about resisting both those temptations by eating with Jesus on the Sabbath—spending Sabbath with him.

RESIST COERCION

In his book *The Three Languages of Politics*, Arnold Kling illustrates a dominant story theme in modern liberal societies—the tale of the oppressed, the oppressor, and the liberator. Today, that story forms the framework of countless new stories. Politically, this story is used to pit one group of people against another. "The rich are oppressing the poor, but if you vote for us, we'll liberate them!" "The government are oppressing the people, but if you vote for us, we'll liberate you!"

Biblically, however, this story isn't about pitting one group of people against another. It's about putting *all* groups of people together with each other and against our *true* enemy.

Just as Pharaoh coerced Israel to do work for him, the devil is quite happy to make us work for him. But our Pharaoh is more subtle, because while we think we're living the dream, we're only tightening our chains. Making more money, raising perfect kids, getting good grades, or even growing great churches or starting successful non-profits are, in our enemy's hands, shackles in disguise.

Every time you look at your Facebook feed and feel that twinge that says, "If you were any kind of success, you'd be doing that/having that/being that/going there"...

Each moment the magazines that line the checkout counter shout, "If you really want to look great, you must do this!"...

... you are being quietly, cunningly coerced to live in a way that you simply do not have to. Dissatisfaction gives way to self-incarceration.

In other words, we are the oppressed. But in this story, the twist is that we are also the oppressors. We're complicit in the demands of the culture around us, even while they crush us. We participate in the pressures placed on us by teachers, parents, politics, and popular moral sensibilities, even while we wish we could be free of them.

A boss pressures her employee to work long hours, even as she wonders how she can cope with the demands of her job.

A father experiences the quiet desperation of discovering that secular dreams never pay out, while insisting that his kids grow up to worship at those same empty altars.

In the rush of the 9-5, we're kept far too busy to see such coercion clearly. Society seeks to coerce you to do far less than God desires. The religious leaders of Jesus' day sought to coerce those round them to do far more. And whether you're on the treadmill of this world seven days a week, or whether one day a week you simply switch treadmills to the one marked "Religious," you never get the chance to lift your head and say, "This is not what it is meant to be about." Following Jesus isn't about swapping your old treadmill for a new one. It's about stepping off of them both.

Embracing the art of rest means declaring each week, "No. I will not live as my society demands, but as my Savior desires." Rest forces us to face questions that may unearth our deep mistrust of God.

"Shall I run after a career to please my boss or shall I embrace rest to please my Savior?"

"Will I worry about promotion or trust God to provide?"

"Will my kids play for one more sports team or will I rely on God to grow and use their gifts?"

"Who is Lord of my Sabbath?"

These are not necessarily easy questions to face, but only by stopping long enough to actually reflect on them will we ever find the answers.

RESIST IDOLATRY
Every problem started with a worship problem.

Think about it. If our world was worshiping God as we ought to, the stress and anxiety of modern life would be altogether different. But decisions are hard, in part, because idols are loud, popular, and demanding. Ancient pagan deities like Baal and Asheroth weren't deplorable to God merely because they were false gods. They were abominations because of what they demanded—sexual immorality, self-harm, and even child sacrifice.

And our modern idols are no less merciless.

Money demands endless work, and control demands harmful, ceaseless worry. Body and beauty cry out for loveless sexual fulfillment. And perhaps the most powerful god of the West—the one in the mirror—demands a complete autonomy which has so often cost the children of such radical individuals their futures, their fathers, and sometimes, their lives. Idol worship is not just displeasing to God (terrible though that is); sooner or later, the false god consumes the worshiper, too.

When the Pharisees rebuked Jesus for his Sabbath sins, they likely thought they were serving God. But they weren't. And Jesus is a genius because, in his answer to the Pharisees, he not only corrected their doctrine but he exposed their idol. Pharisees were Jewish religious nationalists. That's probably why Jesus rebuked them by using their national hero, David:

> [3] *Have you not read what David did when he was hungry, he and those who were with him:* [4] *how he entered the house of God and took and ate the bread of the Presence, which is not lawful for any but the priests to eat, and also gave it to those with him? (Luke 6 v 3-4)*

King David was to Pharisees what George Washington is to American patriots. By invoking their hero, Jesus let them know that he knew what they were living for—more Jewish nationalism than biblical faithfulness. Saying to them, *Your own hero David broke your own Sabbath rules* was like revealing that Washington had warm feelings for the British during the revolution. But Jesus isn't saying this to upset them (that's just a by-product), but to expose them in their idolatry.

And we need him to expose ours, too.

Here it is: whatever it is that you're thinking about right now that gets you off the hook of taking Jesus' call to rest seriously, it is probably the thing you actually love and worship more than Jesus. We refuse rest because, at some deep level, we're convinced that if we stop, the thing for which we're really living won't be fed, pleased, or procured. If you're happier at work than in Christ, rest will never feel good. If you're more of a mother to your children than you are a daughter of the King, stopping may feel like sin.

I know the demands of life are great—young children, a growing company, an ageing parent. But Jesus placed no asterisk next to his words, "The Son of Man is lord of the Sabbath."

Make less money but make more of Christ.

Tell your daughter no so that she can see you say yes to God.

Jesus is the one who has accomplished the greatest of works in order to invite us into his rest. No other god loves you unconditionally. No other god died for you. By inviting us to rest with him, he is inviting us to trust that his rewards are better than our idols', and his peace is better than anything for which we can work.

TAKING UP ARMS

So, how do we do it? How do we rest in such a way that we unseat idols, kick out coercion, resist autonomy, and trade our anxiety for peace?

First, we must embrace levity and leisure. Anxious people just aren't fun. When I'm taking myself too seriously, I can't play with my kids. So on my days of rest, I like to laugh—a lot. Rest is meant to remind us that we are, as Brueggemann said, on the receiving end of God's gifts. That is an incredibly peace-giving, life-infusing reality when it is remembered.

The second essential part of rest is liturgical regularity. If you insist that you'll only rest when you feel like it or on your own terms, you're still the boss. So, submit yourself to a regular pattern of rest, and that pattern of regular surrender of your schedule will start to uproot rebellious autonomy. Like a garden regularly weeded, your soul won't become overgrown with the thorns and thistles of control.

Third, do non-work. Rest offers us a way to resist the coercive controls around us by doing non-work, just for fun. So as you rest, embrace an avocation. Avocation is just a fancy word for hobby—something you do to rest that isn't your job. I like to build things around the house. It's restful for me because it's not my 9-5. I like to go running too. If you told me that I was going to have a small group on my day of rest, I would probably feel less thrilled, because I'm a pastor.

Now maybe that sounds crazy. "You want me to get a hobby?! Do you know how busy I am?" If you're like me, you have reasonable-sounding excuses:

"I have a job with a lot of responsibilities, a wife I'm trying to love, kids I'm trying to raise, neighbors I'm trying to reach, younger men I'm trying to disciple, and you want me to pick up karate?!"

Yes, I want you to pick up karate. Or wood-carving. Or whatever. Because while you're really important, you're not so important that you can't stop. You're like me. You're like any Western man or woman who wants to follow Jesus and thinks that means doing more and more and more. And, you're wrong. You are freed (and commanded) to rest. So pick a few of those things and use the most powerful word in your lexical arsenal: no. It is no sin to say no to a good thing so that you can say yes to the right thing.

Fourth and finally, regularly worship. Ultimately, rest is an act of resistance against the siren calls of our idols to work for them. By stopping, we take up arms against the great Western gods of achievement, money, and self-determination. So when you rest, worship. I'm always a little amazed at how many people I counsel about rest, but who never open their Bibles on their day off. The art of rest is about learning how to rest with Jesus, not from Jesus.

WHAT ARE YOU WORKING FOR?

All work will be done for one of these two ends: to glorify God or to justify us. The same is true for rest.

So, what are you working for? And if you're resting, what are you resting for? Is your life about your ten lonely seconds to justify your whole existence? Are you filled with the anxiety that accompanies the restless service of your idols? I have good news for you: God will never let you miss out on what is truly reward, and he will never withhold from you what is truly good.

That's why Eric Liddell could run so hard and enjoy every step. His race was worship, its result was not all-important, and so his work, and his rest, could be peaceful.

Now, I know what you're thinking:

"Yes, yes. Rest is important. But how!? I work five days a week. I serve at church. I take my kids to their games. How do I do what you're asking?"

We will get there. For now, just remember our working definition: *Sabbath is a time of rest, holy to the Lord.* And you need to want it before you'll really do it. It's about remembering. It's about resisting irreligious autonomy and religious rule-making.

Those are two great reasons to want to let Jesus be Lord of your rest. And there are still two more to come.

4. REST RESTORES RELATIONSHIPS

"Dads have too many tomorrows."
Anonymous

"**G**uys, I need you to clean up your game so we can get going."

I said it in the sweetest dad voice I could muster, but underneath I was all salt and fizz. I had to get to work, I was still cleaning up breakfast, the kids needed to get to school, and they had broken the cardinal rule: NO GAMES BEFORE SCHOOL. The room that had been tidy just moments earlier now wasn't, and I could hear the sounds of many hands and many toys rattling around the room.

Five minutes went by, and there was far too much laughter for any actual cleaning up to be happening.

"GUYS!"

Tone elevated, volume at fortissimo. They looked back at me, half smiling because they were having fun, and half bothered because clearly I was about to ruin it.

"CLEAN UP!"

Why didn't they understand that this was a crazy day? This was not just a normal school-and-work day. This was Wednesday—the weekly school/work/sports/youth group/right-after-the-kids-go-to-bed-I-have-a-pastoral-meeting day. Lagging five minutes late at the beginning would only make every other part of this tightly scheduled day late, too.

They didn't clean up fully, but I had to get going. I sent them upstairs to finish getting ready and yelled up to Hope, "I have to go now!"

I grabbed my bag and shut the door more firmly than necessary. Not a full slam, but with frustrated force.

That day, work wasn't lovely. It was a staccato of serious conversations, budgets, and emails, all to be crammed in before the rushed handover between my wife and me of our four small humans. I didn't get it all done, but when it was time to meet them, I grabbed my bag again and shut the office door with an I-want-you-to-know-I'm-unhappy" semi-bang.

The middle pair of my four kids were late for sports. Tears. The eldest was late to youth group. Eye roll. The smallest was late to nothing because he was endlessly shouting a "song" that he felt everyone on the street definitely needed to hear. It all ended, and somewhere in there they were all fed, and we headed home. On the way to the car, an argument started among them. "Hurry up and get in the car!" I demanded, speaking over the din of their disagreement. I grabbed my bag and threw it on the driver's seat and shut the car door.

Full slam.

We arrived home, and the wrangling toward bed began. Pushing past my own frustration, I decided to try to spend a good moment with them before they laid down for the evening. But then I looked at my watch... late for the meeting. Torn, I decided we would have an "abbreviated" special time.

Turns out it was neither special, nor was there very much time. It was a hurried mash-up of prayers and "How are you?" questions with a face that said, "But tell me quickly because I'm already late for my next meeting." Even if my kids wanted to look past my shouty, anxious herding of them that day and actually tell me anything, I didn't have time to listen.

As I left my house, I shut the door quietly because, for some reason, the moment of its closure was accompanied by a horrible clarity. I realized that I was going to ruin my kids if I didn't stop. Now late for my meeting, I'm not sure I was much help to the man I was counselling, either.

THE MURMUR

Maybe that story sounds fairly familiar to you. Maybe that's why you've picked up this book. The pace of modern life is, by all accounts, dizzying. Multiple 24-hour-news channels, social-media streams, notifications, and good old-fashioned personal interruptions mean that staying focused in the 21st century requires more intentionality than in the 20th.

We just can't get it all done. We can't be informed enough, rich enough, or successful enough.

Busyness bears down on us. Work busyness, family busyness, student busyness, church busyness, and friend busyness are a bunch of fast-talking, complaining customers at the lunch table of your life, working up to fever pitch to get your attention.

And doors end up being slammed because there's just too much.

But if we have ears to hear, we'll listen to those percussive protests and hear them as warnings that all too often, all too easily, and all too unnoticed, our busyness pushes others away from us, and us away from God.

Judith Shulevitz noticed the ruinous rush of modern life. It was in a sermon titled *Work and Rest* by Dr. Tim Keller that I first heard of her. Struck by his observations on our often-unhealthy relationship with work—and her reflections on the sabbath—I decided to pick up her book, too. Living in fast-paced New York City, at some point Shulevitz found that the rush had caught up with her. After returning to her Jewish roots in response, she discovered that, in Sabbath, "not only did drudgery give way to festivity, family gatherings and occasionally worship, but the machinery of self-censorship shut down, too, stilling the eternal inner murmur of self-reproach."[1] As if describing my Wednesdays, she wrote in her book *The Sabbath World: Glimpses of a Different Order of Time*:

> *Like anyone else trying to get ahead, before I had children I logged late hours and weekends in the office, then complained proudly to my friends. When my children were little, I rushed irritably through every diaper change, every walk, every meal. There seemed no other way to retain economic independence, professional viability, a feeling of competence, the faith that I would continue to exist once I stepped outside the house. Observing the Sabbath as it was supposed to be observed seemed strictly aspirational.*

The "eternal inner murmur of self-reproach" that Shulevitz heard is simply the noise that sin makes as it echoes around our hearts. Past mistakes haunt us with a cocktail of guilt and conviction. Past wounds scar with shame. Present shortcomings speak to us of ongoing failure.

---

[1] nytimes.com/2003/03/02/magazine/bring-back-the-sabbath.html. Accessed 12/1/17.

What are your inner murmurs? Well, imagine your top three time commitments suddenly disappeared. Now ask yourself: who would you be? If there were no more school, or work, or spouse, or church activities, and you were left to simply see yourself, what would you see? Would you run from what you see? Those may be the murmurs—the sounds of sins committed by you and to you that you'll do just about anything to escape. They are your insecurities, your fears, and your dark motivations, which send you into great effort at full speed.

After all, what better distraction is there from the feelings and fears of those mistakes, wounds, anxieties, and worries—those inner murmurs—than rushing through life, even at the cost of never really living it? But the very things we do to silence the inner murmurs only end up amplifying them. Dead marriages, distant children, and fair-weather friendships all lie in the wake of the Western wanderer and their quest to quiet the inner voice and find the end-point of the pursuit of happiness.

When we cover the murmurs with the noise of our rushing—when we fail to stop because we don't know what, other than those murmurs, will be left if we pause—it corrodes our relationships. Why? Because relationships require rest; and rest restores relationships.

ROOM FOR RELATIONSHIPS

Rest creates relational room—the space to relate to God and others, the oxygen those relationships require to live and to grow. And yet it is entirely possibly to "do" Sabbath really well, and miss the relationship part.

When I first began to practice the art of rest, I wrote a schedule for my new, weekly Sabbath day. Deciding that I would rest like the best, I created a list, complete with tick-boxes, and worked my plan. If a kid got in the way of a moment's activity like prayer, reading, or working out, they had to be politely shooed away. If my wife wanted to share an idea but it wasn't on my agenda, I would tell her to ask me later. Didn't these people understand that I was trying to rest?

Yeah, I know. It's embarrassing. But I only tell you about my failings to help you see that resting just right isn't exactly the point. That's why we haven't talked about all the details of your own rest implementation yet. Just like going to church, reading the Bible, and attending pot-luck dinners does not a Christian make, regular rest does not good relationships make. But at the same time, without rest, relationships won't have room to grow. Rest is a requirement of, but not a guarantee of, good relationships.

For all his flaws, King David seemed to understand that it took time to develop a relationship with God. His songs are filled with honest and searching prayers, grateful praise, deep longing, and repentant confession.

How could David have created so much masterful poetry about God? He gave it the time it required. Writing poetry from the bottom of your heart does not happen in a snatched thirty seconds as your key turns in the door or as you pray before rushing through your meal. I imagine that for David, it started with the many days he spent on a Judean hillside, simply being with God. At the end of a day of moving the flock, who was his companion? In the fearful moment before confronting a wolf or a bear, who was his back-up? Such experiences doubtless led to his ability to pen such words as Psalm 116:

> ¹ I love the LORD, because he has heard my voice and my pleas for mercy.
> ² Because he inclined his ear to me,
>   therefore I will call on him as long as I live.
> ³ The snares of death encompassed me;
>   the pangs of Sheol laid hold on me;
>   I suffered distress and anguish.
> ⁴ Then I called on the name of the LORD:
>   "O LORD, I pray, deliver my soul!"
>
> ⁵ Gracious is the LORD, and righteous;
>   our God is merciful.
> ⁶ The LORD preserves the simple;
>   when I was brought low, he saved me.
> ⁷ Return, O my soul, to your rest;
>   for the LORD has dealt bountifully with you. (v 1-7)

It is a great and glorious truth that we humans were made for the glory of God. To experience and express all the wonders of his manifold attributes is the delightful vocation of his people.

And we express the glory of God as we experience relationship with God. We won't declare him if we do not know him. But if we never have any time to enjoy being with him—if we're never resting with him—then what have we to express to the world? "Come meet Jesus! I barely have time to be with him, but trust me, he's great."

After all, aren't our human relationships like that? If I only managed my household with my wife and never had time to simply enjoy spending time with her, how good would our relationship really be? If I shuttle my kids from school to sports, or music lessons to youth group, but never stop all that activity to just be with them, what kind of relationship will I have with them when they don't need me like that anymore?

Of course I spend time with my God as I walk through the to-do list of my day, just as I am with my kids as I drive them places, and with my wife as we seek to herd the kids to bed. But if that is the only way I am spending time with God, can I be surprised if my relationship with him feels functional and transactional rather than delightful and natural?

HOW (NOT) TO SILENCE THE INNER MURMUR

But still, there's that inner murmur. It needs quieting if I am to invest in my relationships rather than enduring them or using them. Here are a few common ways I've found myself trying to silence my own personal inner-prosecutor:

1. Bad Work

Nothing helps me to not deal with my own issues like seeking to drown them in a sea of to-do's. The trouble is, my issues float. If I hear the little voice in my head tell me that I'm not enough, then I'll work extra hard to silence it.

I'm *great* at this. Personally, my preference for work isn't about proving wrong the inner murmur of my own self-reproach, but about forgetting it's even there in the first place. By flitting about from duty to duty, my relationships with God and others—relationships that would cause me to face my own inner murmurs—are ignored.

2. Shallow Relationships

How much of my life has been spent trying to satisfy a deep longing with a shallow solution? The desire to be liked, popular, and praised supplants the practices of deep, unhurried love. Social media instead of deep conversation. Silently smiling through Instagram feeds instead of the story of shared memory with others. Shallow relationships appear to be pain-free ways to scratch the itch of intimacy, while never curing the deeper disorder.

3. Misusing Rest

Expensive vacations, lazy mornings, and spending money on myself become not about setting apart special time to relate to God and others, but to stuff myself with the goods and services of this world. Consumption shouts louder than that murmur—but it quiets down quickly. And when we pursue our me-moments, it usually comes at the expense of others. The boss, the beautician, the maid, the exploited worker in another country... these people need to get out of our way and get into helping us serve ourselves, right?

4. Emptying Yourself

In Eastern spirituality, the main point of meditation and silence is to empty yourself of yourself. In practices like yoga, mindfulness, and directed meditation, well-meaning Westerners engage in a series of activities that, they imagine, will silence the inner voice by convincing them it's not there. Or more accurately, that they're not there.

All of these activities carry with them a promise to silence the insistent echoes of the reality of our sin. And, for a while—maybe even a long while—they seem to work. But while they can temporarily drown out the noise, they can't make it go away. These practices may drown out the voice, but they never replace it.

Only time to be with and enjoy God, who sees those depths and loves us just the same, can do that.

RELATING TO GOD THROUGH REST

The words of David help us shape our practice of relational rest. Here are a few ways they counter those common mistakes we just talked about:

1. *Gracious Rest (Not Bad Work)*

> *I love the LORD, because he has heard my voice and my pleas for mercy.*
> *Because he inclined his ear to me,*
> *therefore I will call on him as long as I live.*

While work offers us a screen of endless distraction, God is inviting us to rest with him.

"But I'm not done," we say. "There's so much to do. I've not made myself ready."

And you're probably right. But notice that David doesn't say, "I love the Lord because he accepted my great shepherding." Or, "I love the Lord, now that this whole running-the-country thing is under control." He loves the Lord because God hears, God listens, and God inclines himself toward David.

We don't have to wait until the work is done to rest with God. Our personal sense of accomplishment isn't what we bring to God; it's what we're meant to get from him.

Slow down and meditate on that last sentence. Your sense of security and accomplishment is not the ticket you must present to God in order to relate to him. Relationship is the gift he wishes to present to you, to be enjoyed regularly as you simply come to him. No wonder David could say that he loved God! He was heard in his relationship with him, so he didn't have to prove anything to him.

2. Deep Fellowship (Not Shallow Relationships)

Gracious is the LORD, and righteous;
our God is merciful.
The LORD preserves the simple;
when I was brought low, he saved me.

Shallow relationships are exhausting because they require the maintenance of an image. Yet, when I can truly pour my heart out to God or a godly friend, then I experience mercy, closeness, and salvation. When David reflects how "when I was brought low, he saved me," he's talking about humiliation. People before whom you may be truly humiliated and loved simultaneously are the kind of people you keep.

But such deep fellowship with God and others can't be microwaved. It takes time. And when we carve out the time, we're rewarded with the relational fellowship for which we were made. We find ourselves loving to carve out the time to focus on our relationship, rather than having to do so. Duty gives way to delight.

3. Sharing Moments (Not Misusing Rest)

Return, O my soul, to your rest;
for the LORD has dealt bountifully with you.

There is a danger in writing a book about rest to Western people, because we may think that rest is all about us. "Let me get good and rested," we may tell ourselves, "and then I'll get out there and relate to others." "I deserve a rest; I've done well this week." Yet, that is not the framework of the Bible. Scripture never commands us to disengage relationally in order to be truly refreshed. Neither does it dangle rest as something that is there for us, as our earned wages after a busy day or week. Rather, it commands us to press into deeper relationship with God and others and, in doing so, to find our healing.

4. Being Refilled (Not Emptying Yourself)

> *The snares of death encompassed me;*
> * the pangs of Sheol laid hold on me;*
> * I suffered distress and anguish.*
> *Then I called on the name of the LORD:*
> * "O LORD, I pray, deliver my soul!"*

The problems of life are real, not imaginary. Eastern meditation starts with the presupposition that pain in this world is illusory, but the gospel tells us that we don't have to pretend that what hurts does not, or should not. Life does hurt. Yet the gospel doesn't leave us there. Rest with God grows our ability to say, "I know God, and I know he will deliver me." It enables us to face problems with both honesty and hope.

RUSHING RUINS RELATIONSHIPS

David loved the Lord because he knew God heard him. Do you know that? I mean, I know you probably agree with the claim—but do you know it?

Recently, I had to correct one of my daughters. For this particular child, the process of loving correction and repentance takes a long time. She loves to share her thoughts and talk through her problems. But that creates a problem for me, because this requires what I so often don't want to give—time. So in this conversation, she was speaking her mind and baring her soul... and I could feel all that salt and fizz rising again. And after a while I could bear it no more. I looked at her and said,

"Listen, I love you, but you've got to speed this up."

I knew straightaway I shouldn't have said it.

Tears welled in her eyes. I apologized, but the damage was done. She said, "Dad, do you even have time to hear me?"

The good news is that God is a great dad, where I am a mediocre one, and my Father forgives my kids' father for every one of his failures. God hears us, if we will take time to pour ourselves out before him. God speaks to us, if we will take time to hear him. God loves us, and we need to take time to know that. And yet how often we consider the idea of carving out time to grow our relationship with God, and think through what that might look like, and still say,

"Listen God, I love you, but you've got to speed this up."

So here's a question: do you really want to have a relationship with God, or do you just want to have business transactions with him? We were made for relationship with him, and everything he has done for us in Christ will one day bring us into such closeness with him that we see him face to face and never want to turn away. We will know him even as we are fully known by him (1 Corinthians 13 v 12).

The question we have to ask ourselves is: how surprising do I want that experience to be? Will I ensure that the daily rhythm of my life is one that will make that glorious experience the natural endpoint of a life that was lived in relationship with him? Or will meeting him on that future day be so jarring and utterly different from my experience with him now that I'm at best unprepared for it or, worse, among those who turn out to have spent their lives so relationally disconnected from God that they find themselves without a relationship with him at all in the future?

Look, not taking a Sabbath break doesn't make you lose your salvation. That's a silly idea. But never bothering to make time to rest with God should make you at least begin to ask yourself whether you have really ever experienced salvation—whether you really know him in the first place.

CONVERSATIONS WITH MY FATHER

God is a great dad. And like any great dad, his kids want to hang out with him. So, here are four questions I want you to ask yourself to help you chart out the art of rest yourself.

First, ask yourself if you're really interested in having a relationship with God. Don't skip past that question— really think on it. Do you want to know God deeply, having his word and his Spirit penetrating the lowest parts of your soul? Do you truly want to be heard by him, and to hear him in return? Yes? Well, then you're going to pursue and prioritize such a life.

Second, ask yourself where rushing is ruining your relationships with God and others. What decisions need to be made today in order to resist the rush, and rest in relationship with God? This question affects our daily practices and our weekly rhythms, so don't be afraid. The answers may surprise you.

Third, in what unhealthy ways have you tried to silence your own inner murmur of self-reproach? What will change if you grasp the truth that it is the forgiveness of our heavenly Father that silences that murmur, and it is rest with him that fills the quiet with the sound of conversation between Father and child?

Fourth, will you stop waiting to rest? Go ahead and pull out your calendar and begin to consider where you can put in regular moments of rest with God—moments in a day, an hour in a morning, a day in the week, as you're able to. Start to jot down how, given what we've learned so far, you'll shape those times—that hour, or that day, with God. What will you do? What will you not do? With whom will some of those moments be shared, and what might that do to strengthen those relationships, too?

As we engage in the work of pushing back all the ways we try to silence our own inner murmurs, this I can promise you: God will meet you. You've not ruined your capacity to rest with God. No matter how many doors you've slammed, kids you've rushed, times you've failed, or deadlines you've missed, God is not impatient. He is waiting for you in your moments of rest because he himself is the One our rest is for. He longs to relate to us so deeply that we can say,

"I love the Lord, because I know he hears me."

5. REST BRINGS REWARD

"And which of you by being anxious can add
a single hour to his span of life?"
Jesus (Matthew 6 v 27)

The most tragic people in the airport are the runners.

They run, usually in business clothes, dragging their life on wheels behind them, to catch their flight, which they often miss.

Many times, I've been the tragic airport runner. I have a gift for missing flights. The anxiety is real. I think, "I need to catch my flight. I have work to do. It's important that I'm not delayed. Things will kinda fall apart if I am." All of these thoughts swirl around my head. Blood pressure increases, annoyance is palpable, and trusting-God me and still-trusting-myself me come into contact once again.

Yet all my frustration never helps me make my connection. I'm just dragging my bags, hurriedly but (in my case) inevitably missing my destination.

That's the runners. Then there's another group—never hurried, and actually seeming to enjoy the experience. They are the most triumphant people in the airport: the diners.

They eat, drink, and enjoy a good conversation or a book at one of the many restaurants or bars in the terminal. And when a tragic runner rushes past a triumphant diner, the diner understands—they've probably run through the airport, too, in the past.

The diner still has to catch his flight—but they have found a way to enjoy the journey by taking a break. The journey offers a bit of a reward to the diner. They've beaten the anxiety of the airport by creating a moment to rest. That is, they have come to realize that on the journey there is a way to have time to board the plane and time to relax along the way.

The metaphor isn't perfect, of course, but if life is an airport then far too many of us are rushing through its terminals. Far too many of us are locked in "runner mode." Yet in rest we are offered rewards on the journey itself. Rest anticipates the destination along the journey, because it offers an experience akin to being at the destination even while we are on the journey. For Christians, space to pause and be with God—the God we're walking towards as we travel through this life—offers generous rewards.

NO MORE EXCUSES

I know you have great reasons to rush. Me too. So let's just agree that we're really busy, and that our busyness will no longer keep us from the rewards God offers to us through rest. I've often thought, "If God wants me to rest, then why has he put me in such restless situations?" Pages could be filled with the busy barriers between me and rest's rewards, just as they could, I'm sure, for you. But I want the rewards offered by holy rest. God wants them for me too, because he's a God who loves to give good things.

Christians can get all bent out of shape trying to figure out the will of God. But Scripture is pretty silent on God's will in the specific situations of our particular lives. So, let me give you a more helpful concept: God's disposition. God's secret counsels are just that—secret. "Who has known the mind of the Lord?" (Romans 11 v 34). But God's disposition... that's as plain as the book you're reading. He really, really, really loves his people. And, he really, really, really loves to give us good gifts:

> Fear not, little flock, for it is your Father's good
> pleasure to give you the kingdom. (Luke 12 v 32)

We simply really struggle to trust him on this one—that God loves to give us life in his perfect kingdom, the joys of knowing him as our gracious Lord, now and forever.

We don't trust that he actually desires to give us rest now and rest later. We struggle to believe that he likes to give us lazy Saturdays, laughter with friends, delicious food, and deep moments of prayer.

But stop and re-read the words of Jesus. God takes pleasure in giving us the kingdom. Don't you think that means he might also take pleasure in giving you a break?

God has gifts for us waiting in real rest, so let's see what a few of them are.

THE REWARD OF MEMORY

Most nights I have what is called "special time" with my kids. We spend a moment reading the Bible together, talking about the day, and connecting. As my kids have gotten older, it's changed. Reading from children's story Bibles has morphed into talking about deep theological questions. Prayers have gone from "God help me have a happy heart" into the deeper longings of the human soul. But one thing that has never changed is the question I ask them every time, just before we end.

"Who are you?" I ask.

"I am a man of God, dad," say my sons.

"I'm a woman of God," say my daughters.

The human soul has an entropic relationship with identity—that is, we slowly forget who we are. So we need to be reminded. I've addressed this already in chapter two, but that's my point: I need to address it again, because I'll bet that since you read that chapter, like me since I wrote that chapter, you have not remembered what is in that chapter. We just keep forgetting who we are in relationship to our Father.

For each of my children, a special time each day to talk, listen, and connect affords us both the gift of memory. This gift battles in our soul's inherent entropy. And if I, a very mediocre father, can gift my children in this way in our restful moments, how much more can our heavenly Father do so for us?

The author of Hebrews draws out this important connection. In chapters 3 and 4, he compares Israel's forty years in the desert to the journey of professing Christians through this life. As we have seen, part of Israel's problem was that they kept violating God's Sabbath commands, and in doing so they forgot who they were—and failed to enter the true rest of the promised land (Hebrews 3 v 11). Starting a journey is not much use if you forget where you're going and never make it to the destination. And so the writer encourages—and challenges—his readers:

> For we have come to share in Christ, if indeed we hold our original confidence firm to the end. (Hebrews 3 v 14)

That's a strange sentence. The first part, "For we have come to share in Christ," is in the past tense, as if it were already done. But then comes the conditional, "if." "If indeed we hold our original confidence firm to the end," is about the future. So we are left to conclude that our future faithfulness secures our past share in Christ. Put simply, we came to share in Christ through past faith if we continue to be faithful till we reach the "end," and the destination of eternity.

So I must hold my original confidence. I must not forget who I am. And how do I hold on? By ensuring that I make the time to pause and think about it.

In the first chapter we noted one of the devil's greatest schemes: to keep us from entering the "time-temple" and enjoying rest with God. Here, we're making a similar observation. The great C.S. Lewis put this very scheme into the mouth of Wormwood, the senior devil in his masterful book *The Screwtape Letters*:

> *Do everything in your power to keep your patient from regular communion with our Enemy, and convince him that being busy in life and ministry is an acceptable excuse not to spend regular time in prayer.*

God wants to give you the reward of memory. And he is asking you, "Who are you?" Do you have time to slow down, reflect, and give him (and remind yourself of) the answer?

THE REWARD OF REFLECTION

Working ceaselessly means you never have the chance to think deeply.

So much of our work, our speech, and our habits are formed in the routines of life. And it's while going through those routines that we usually become aware of how we'd like to be different. We'd like to pray more, workout some, or start eating better. Yet because we have not yet mastered the art of rest, we don't experience the reward of deep reflection.

In the world, reflection is the privilege of the elite who don't have to work so hard. Like the philosopher-kings of the great Greek thinker Plato, only the few get the chance to step back and think upon life, meaning, and the cosmos. But it was never meant to be this way in the kingdom of God.

When God rescued Israel from slavery and gave them the Sabbath, he universalized rest. The gift of time to reflect was available to all, regardless of education, vocation, or financial success. Sabbath was Israel's liberation not just from false gods, but from living as though they worshiped false gods. Our God created humans to image him—to do what he does. And part of the glory of image-bearing is enjoying the reward of reflecting on that fact, and on how we can enjoy being more like him.

This is a gift he graciously gives to all his people. It's up to us whether or not we shall receive it.

Imagine a people who love God deeply, not only reflexively. I know that some of God's people think and feel deeply, but many of us rush through scrambled, frenetic lives on the school run, in church meetings, taking on community responsibilities, changing diapers, and so on, and so on. People like that go to church, sure. They may even attend a small group. But what if, *en masse*, they stopped regularly to think,

"How am I doing with living in God's image, becoming more like Jesus, embodying the new world?"

"When, and how, will I need consciously to rely on God today?"

Simply pausing to reflect creates the soul-space into which the Holy Spirit can speak to his people. That's what rest offers.

THE REWARD OF SECURITY

The author of Hebrews encourages us to "strive to enter that rest" that will be ours when we reach our promised land (4 v 11). But I would argue that the inverse is also important: we must rest on our journey there to remember why we're striving.

When the people of Israel were freed from their slavery in Egypt, they were fully redeemed by God. Before they received the law, before they journeyed, before they built the tabernacle, God set his saving, adopting love upon them. When they were nothing—minority slaves of an ancient superpower, facing ethnic extinction within two generations—God made them something: something more than any of them could have imagined.

It was after they were delivered from Egypt that God gave them laws and a tabernacle—not before. What does this mean?

In the verse before Hebrews 4 v 11 (you guessed it—verse 10), the writer speaks of a rest that sounds different than the rest of verse 11:

> *Whoever has entered God's rest has also rested from his works as God did from his.*

Slaves can't rest. Slaves can't take a day off to recuperate, reflect, and enjoy God. Slaves must work—either to pay off a debt, to please their master, or to simply stay alive.

And most of us are slaves—because we enslave ourselves to the American Dream, the boss, our kids, or even (and worse) to earning God's favor. We're so often working to prove something, or to pay someone, or to get the promotion.

But whoever enters God's "rest" lays down that kind of life-proving work. We have rested from our works. Why? Because suddenly and supernaturally, we are secure. We have been saved apart from our work, regardless of the merit of our work. We have been adopted as children without regard to our achievements.

Only children can rest. Only kids have the security not to feel they need to work for affection or reward. If my kids want to take a day off to enjoy life around the house, eat my food, and hang with me, I'm thrilled!

Why? Because they are my children. I want to be with them. And as my children, they are free to enjoy all that I have. In fact, it's my pleasure that they do. I'm proud to call them mine, honored to be their father, and eager to hear their thoughts. They know that security of that relationship, and they rest in it—and God is a way better dad than I am.

Rest is the privilege of sons, but only the dream of slaves.

And in the gospel, God has called us sons, not slaves:

> [14] *All who are led by the Spirit of God are sons of God.*
> [15] *For you did not receive the spirit of slavery to fall back into fear, but you have received the Spirit of adoption as sons, by whom we cry, "Abba! Father!"*
>
> (Romans 8 v 14-15)

We have the rights and privileges of those who have been adopted into his family, one of which is rest in the secure knowledge that we're loved. For the exodus community, rest memorialized the fact that Egypt was no longer their address, their god was no longer Pharaoh, and they were no longer slaves. Rest offers us the reward of living out the security of our sonship—if we would receive it.

THE REWARD OF ENDURANCE

If anyone had a good reason to be running through the airport of life, it was Jesus. You and I have a lot we must accomplish, but it pales in comparison with the work facing him. Making a deadline is one thing; making a way for sinners to be saved is quite another. Add to that the fact that he only really began work on such a project in his final three years of life here, and you'd think Jesus would have been an anxiety attack in sandals, and that taking time out would have been out of the question.

And yet...

> *Jesus often withdrew to lonely places and prayed.*
> *(Luke 5 v 16, NIV)*

> *[He] went up on the mountain by himself to pray. When evening came, he was there alone... (Matthew 14 v 23)*

> *In these days he went out to the mountain to pray, and all night he continued in prayer to God. (Luke 6 v 12)*

Jesus had so much to do that he made sure he stopped to sit with his Father. Why? Because he understood that moments of holy rest offer the reward of endurance. If we want to keep going, we need to keep stopping.

Physically, we get this. Our bodies get tired, so we sleep. If I refuse sleep on the basis that I need to train for a marathon, I will fail to run a marathon, because my body needs rest in order to train. So why would we think it should be all that different with our souls? When our souls are tired, why wouldn't we rest? Jesus seems to have made a habit of this. Are we a bit more spiritually fit than the Lord?

Jesus cares about our rest. After he sent his own disciples out on their first mission trip, they returned full of excitement. You can imagine a dozen guys, most likely aged between 16 and 20, clamoring to tell their teacher about the miracles, the healings, and the crazy exorcisms they just saw. What was Jesus' response? "Come away by yourselves to a desolate place and rest a while" (Mark 6 v 30-31). Even at their young, energetic age, Jesus wanted them to enjoy the rewards not only of a job well done, but a rest well taken.

If we would endure, we must rest. Working really hard without rest is a good way to achieve a lot in the short term, followed by dropping out or burning out. Hard work that is regularly punctuated by deep rest is the way to achieve your purpose in the long term. You may have decades of great things ahead of you in this life. You need to rest along the way.

THE REWARD OF ANTICIPATION

Running through life's airport doesn't get you to the destination faster. The time of your departure is already fixed, and not by you (Psalm 139 v 16). And you must keep walking till that day. As the author of Hebrews puts it, you must "strive to enter that rest" (Hebrews 4 v 11). In God's future world, we will be rewarded with the great gift, the perfect rest, of consummation—the full union of heaven and earth, and the peaceful pleasure of that new reality. In this life, rest does not give us the gift of consummation—but it does offer us the gift of anticipation.

Think of this: if rest is merely the break between toil, that's fine enough. But since rest is meant to be more than that—a time holy to the Lord—it's infused with a deeper significance. Rest with God in this life points us forward to the ultimate rest with God beyond this life. Rest leaves us with a little tinge of anticipation, as if it wasn't quite the break we were aiming for. That's because it's not.

In a personal letter to a friend, C.S. Lewis wrote:

> All joy (as distinct from mere pleasure, still more amusement) emphasizes our pilgrim status: always reminds, beckons, awakes desire. Our best havings are wantings.

The joy of a peaceful break, a wonderful Sabbath, or a refreshing time of prayer are bigger than themselves. Having such rest reorients our hopes for the day when we have the better thing—the restful presence of God himself, forever.

We don't often consider an anticipation a reward, but a torment. Waiting for Christmas was the scourge of childhood. Waiting for the promotion, for the wedding day, for the bonus, for the child to arrive—waiting is a tough business. And yet, the waiting made the having special, didn't it?

In stories, the build-up of the plot makes the moment it all comes together at the end even more special. Human history is no different. God has written an eons-long story of his creativity, power, love, and grace. And when his Son returns to draw that story to a close and set this world right again, all our small moments of rest will make sense. They will have oriented our hearts just a bit more toward that moment for which we were made: to be with him fully, with hearts and faces unveiled.

QUIT RUNNING THROUGH THE TERMINAL

So, quit running.

Frenetic travelers we often are, passing through the terminals of each life stage, running, running, always running for something. Yet if we faithfully embraced the art of rest, we would find ourselves richly rewarded. The journey would be so much better if we created moments to enjoy who we truly are in Christ—giving us good time to reflect on the journey, to be gifted with fresh endurance, and to anticipate all that is to come.

Life is like an airport, and, as the people of God, we have our tickets to the new heavens and earth bought and paid for by Christ. If we travel well, we will make it through the difficult moments of the journey while also being able to enjoy a few foretastes of the destination itself. We can stop to enjoy the rewards of rest because we know God built in the time to do that.

Quit rushing.

You're not late. In Christ, you're on time because you're not on your time. He holds the world together by the word of his power, and he's not going to fall off his throne if you press pause. Let the way you traverse the journey not only be the way you reach the destination, but the way you prepare for and anticipate it. Rest offers us the rewards—we just have to take them. If we do, we'll find our hearts increasingly oriented away from the anxious chains of this world, and free to wonder at the world to come.

6. STARTING TO STOP

"Yesterday is gone.
Tomorrow has not yet come.
We have only today.
Let us begin."
Mother Teresa

So now we get to it—starting to stop.

You've waited the whole book to get to this chapter.

Or, if you've cheated and have just flipped to this chapter because you're so desperate for a break that you just want to know how to begin. Well, if you did do that, after you repent in sackcloth and ashes for dismissing what amounts to a decent amount of work for me (and my editor!), you should go back and read the rest of the book. Why? Because the *why* of rest is just as important as the *how*.

There are a lot of bad reasons to rest: laziness, lack of motivation, or a false reward for a poor job, to name a few. We are not learning the art of rest for any of those. We embrace the art of rest because it is a gift given to us by God, practiced among us by Christ, inspired for us by the Holy Spirit, and inviting us to fellowship with Father, Son, and Spirit. As we say yes to this kind of rest, his refreshing, unburdened, and happy presence will begin to flow into our lives, and therefore into our world.

I've taken a few chapters to explain why God has given us, and commanded us to practice, the art of rest. I did this to soften the ground of your heart so that a good, new set of ideas and practices might grow. If you skip the why, you'll be trying to grow a tree on top of pavement. You'll have better success if you bust up some concrete first.

BETTER THAN LAW-KEEPING

Notice what I have *not* said in this book. I have not concluded that you must rest one day every week, on a Sunday, because that is the way we uphold God's commandments to keep the Sabbath day. I realize that there are many good Christian people who hold this view; I am simply not among them.

Now, if you're convinced from Scripture that it is a matter of obedience to take Sundays as your day of rest, I am going respectfully to disagree with you—but I'm also going to say, "Don't go against your conscience." If, as you read the Scriptures carefully and humbly, this is where you're led, then please follow that leading. But at the same time, let's not divide over this issue. About 96%

of this book you can (and I hope will) still want to agree with, apply, and find liberating.

I am simply making the case here that the Sabbath laws were fulfilled in Christ, which is what a good portion of the book of Hebrews is about (Hebrews 3 – 4), and certainly what Colossians 2 v 16-17 is about:

> [16] *Therefore let no one pass judgment on you in questions of food and drink, or with regard to a festival or a new moon or a Sabbath.* [17] *These are a shadow of the things to come, but the substance belongs to Christ.*

Here, Paul is explicitly commanding us not to get judgmental regarding these matters, including "a Sabbath," because the point isn't the day. The point is the thing to which a Sabbath day *points*—namely, our forever future with God.

It's ironic how so many Christians have carried on anxious debates about Sabbath-keeping practices. Well, that's not what we're after here. Doing no work every Saturday was, for the Jewish believers before Christ came, a sign pointing them to Jesus. As we practice the art of rest, we're free from the specifics of the command (only on Saturdays, always on Saturdays, don't do any form of labor, and so on), but not from the wisdom, the principle, of the command—to embrace regular, holy rest.

Because Jesus is our rest, we can enjoy him whenever we like. And we should! But we must be careful, because saying, "I don't need to take a regular Sabbath because

Jesus is my Sabbath," might just be another way of living your life foolishly committed to overwork and failing to spend proper time with Jesus at all. Just as saying "I'll pray for you" has become for many Christians a substitute for "I don't want to talk with you about this anymore, and I may well not remember to pray for you," so saying we're free not to take a Sabbath day on Sundays (or Saturdays) must never be a cipher for "I am too busy and too idolatrous and too proud to bother to give Jesus any of my time at all."

We are free to engage in rest not as law obedience but as worshipful art form. We are *not* free to ignore God's command and invitation to rest. So what follows in this chapter is not an exegesis of biblical "rest laws." Rather, it is my best attempt to give you biblical wisdom about the art of rest, and how you can implement it in your life.

DAILY, WEEKLY, YEARLY

Imagine you were a Jewish believer in 400 BC and you had a sudden, profound sense of your need to fellowship with God. What must you do? Well, if it wasn't a Saturday, you probably were going to have to wait. Not that you couldn't pray, but you weren't free to linger in his presence and put down your labors, because it wasn't Sabbath time. But as followers of Jesus, we have a level of freedom and access to God of which Old Testament believers could but dream. Pentecost has come, the Spirit has been poured out into the church, and the presence of God is with us right now.

Thus we are more free than we imagine ourselves to be. Why? Because we can work with Spirit-empowered energy, and we are free not only to cease from constant work, but to step into Spirit-saturated fellowship.

I have a friend who practices a daily art of rest in a way that inspires and challenges me. He is a busy guy—the pastor of a fast-growing church, the father of many children, and the husband of a gifted and godly wife. For the first part of his ministry life he would stack his schedule so that he could take his weekly day of rest. Rushing from appointment to appointment, he would arrive at the end of his week at his day of rest feeling that he had drained himself all week.

Tiring of the ragged way he would end up approaching his weekend, my friend made a decision that changed his life. He asked his assistant to build a five-minute space between each one of his meetings for him to pray—and his life changed. Between each counseling appointment, staff meeting, or visit, he would take five minutes to stop, pray, and rest. He would literally pause his day, multiple times per day, simply to rest. Little and often throughout the day, he feasted on the bread of God.

"It's there for the taking, Adam," he told me. "We just have to pause and eat."

My friend is simply embracing what many other Christians have practiced throughout the ages. Some Christians call this the Daily Office. Variations of such practices permeate monastic Christianity, Eastern Orthodoxy, and even modern Christianity. It doesn't really matter what we call it—only that we take note of it. A great first step in starting to stop is to build in small allowances throughout the day to breathe, pray, eat, reflect, and worship. It doesn't have to be much, but it does have to exist.

Along with a daily practice, I think that the Scriptures make a clear pattern for us to rest each week. Where Old Testament laws no longer apply as Christian requirements, they can and should shape the wisdom of Christian practice. I take a day of rest each week, usually on Fridays. As we've seen, it's not about Sunday, but it is about some day. This pattern of weekly rest is not a law command, and therefore not taking one isn't sin. Instead, it's a pattern in creation, in Old Testament law, and a wise idea. Not taking a day of rest each week is not sin—but it's probably stupid.

I realize that there are a million good reasons why taking a weekly day of rest is hard. Medical school, the early stages of motherhood, the starting of a business, or the meeting of a deadline are all good sounding reasons, and may be legitimate exceptions. Mothers of newborns can't take a day away from their children initially. Don't you think God knows that? He did create motherhood (and medicines), after all.

But exceptions are meant to be just that—exceptions: temporary interruptions to what is otherwise an accepted pattern. We are free to flex in the varying seasons and crises of life—but if you flex something for too long, it warps. Flex sometimes, but always move back to the general rhythm of a day of rest each week.

So, pull out your schedule. Try to imagine what life would be like if you were to embrace the practice of weekly rest. The art of rest might just require you practice a sister art that we mentioned briefly in chapter three: the use of the word "no." You don't have to say yes to every ministry opportunity, extracurricular activity, or social event. If you were to take rest more seriously than reputation, and trust God to do his work even when you are not doing yours, I'll bet you'd find that you have an uncanny ability to make time for priorities. I'm also willing to wager that you have more control over your schedule than you'd like to admit. If you'll prayerfully look at the way you spend your time, you'll likely be able to find space for much of what you really want.

Finally, the Scriptures give us a pattern for another form of rest: irregular, jubilee kind of rest (e.g. Exodus 23 v 10-11). In modern parlance, we call this "vacation," "holiday," or "sabbatical."

There are times each year when both my wife and I carve out moments to be alone, to be with God, and to be somewhere else. We stumbled upon this pattern one year when one of my trips changed, leaving me with a few days on my own. Those few days were one of the happiest accidents of my life. Ever since, we've worked to create at least one time each year when she can get away, and one when I can too. What might it look like for you to carve out intentional moments for personal, restful reflection? Setting aside evenings after kids are asleep? Scheduling a personal prayer retreat? Giving your spouse a day off? Here, creativity can abound and make room for rest.

These patterns—daily, weekly, and yearly—form a good start to helping you think about when you might start to practice the art of rest yourself. But they also force us to ask another question: what on earth do we do in that time?

HOW TO REST

I began this book by recounting to you one of the most well-rehearsed fights in my marriage: what to do on our day off. This conversation would always stress me out because Hope would simply say, "Let's just relax," and my wiring means I have no idea how to do that. Thankfully, as Hope began to learn how I function, she began to help me. Maybe you're wondering what to do in your time of not doing? Here are a few ideas. Some of them we mentioned already, in passing:

Sleep
You need rest—literal, physical rest. Most of us don't sleep enough. Whole industries have arisen to solve a problem that most humans in history didn't struggle with: sleep. The range of pillows, mattresses, drugs,

white-noise machines, and therapies just to achieve good sleep is dizzying. Perhaps this has less to do with an inherent physical problem and more to do with a ubiquitous overwork problem.

On your day off, sleep. That's right: take a nap, sleep in, or just go to bed early. The world won't break just because you're not awake. In fact, a good nap can be an act of faith in God's providence. That's what it seemed to be for David when he wrote, "In peace I will both lie down and sleep; for you alone, O LORD, make me dwell in safety" (Psalm 4 v 8).

Read
My early-morning time with the Lord is good, but it's never long enough. Kids always wake up, the day always starts, and at some point I have to close my Bible. When was the last time you gave yourself an hour or two to just sit down and enjoy reading the whole book of, say, Mark? How long has it been since you read the Scriptures not to do the work of study but to enjoy the work of the divine author? A day of rest is a great time to wander through a book in the Bible in deep interest, allowing yourself to experience it and not just study it. Maybe your regular Bible reading is in a rut. Maybe this is a great way to rejuvenate it.

Pray
Just as my daily Bible-reading never feels long enough, so too my daily prayer rarely seems to go deep enough.

Sabbath days are wonderful opportunities to talk and listen in prayer more than we are normally able to. I will often find myself on prayer walks on these days, pouring my mind and heart out to God. Rest allows me to do this, and can allow you to do it too. Maybe you have a great daily prayer life, or maybe you don't. Rest can make room for you to grow here. Jesus took time away from the work to pray—we probably should, too.

Reflect

Have you ever given yourself time to think? The Scriptures use different words for this activity: meditate, ponder, consider... any of them will do. All of them point to an activity not of hurried decision-making but of thoughtful decision-reviewing. One way to reflect is through writing. For me, keeping a journal has allowed reflection, and I would commend the practice for helping you to review your thoughts, emotions, and actions. On your day of rest, taking moments to look over your shoulder can both help you adjust and fill you with faith. Why? Because when we're always consumed by where we need to go, we never get a chance to thank God for where we've been. Reflection fosters gratitude for what God has done and trust for what God will do.

Avocate

The word "avocation" simply describes something one does that isn't your principle vocation. For me, it's building stuff with my hands. I'm a pastor, so I spend most of my week building things with my mind, my words, or my faith. But on my day off I often find it very satisfying to build things with my hands. What do you like to do when you're not doing what you have to do? That's what I mean. God made a great world, and enjoying it is one way we worship him and are moved to praise him (1 Timothy 4 v 4-5), and therefore it is something he enjoys watching us do.

Recreate

Like avocation, recreation is an activity. But unlike avocation, recreation is purely playful. You're not building, you're bonding. While there is some overlap between avocation and recreation, recreation usually describes relief from toil by doing something fun. The word literally means "to make anew." Holy rest should do that for us—refresh us enough to get back to work. God is a hilarious, life-filled, joyful God. He likes us, and likes to see us have good fun.

Eat

I am so glad God made food. Think about how extravagantly good that gift is. God could have created us to eat, but not taste. Or, not taste well. He could have filled our bodies with chlorophyll so we'd photosynthesize. But God gave us this great gift of food. On your day off, enjoy food. In your times of rest, gather with others around a meal. Even the skeptical teacher of Ecclesiastes sees that great food is a wonderful gift:

> ^{24} *There is nothing better for a person than that he*
> *should eat and drink and find enjoyment in his toil.*
> *This also, I saw, is from the hand of God,* ^{25} *for apart*
> *from him who can eat or who can have enjoyment?*
> (Ecclesiastes 2 v 24-25)

Sing

Maybe you're not all that musical, but I bet you sing. Maybe it's when you're in the car alone, or when you're in the shower, or when you're doing some chores in the house. We all do it, even if not all of us "can sing." Once a week, my family gathers around the piano and we sing. Like an old Puritan household, we open hymnals and sing anthems of our faith. At other times we blast the latest worship album as loud as we can and host a no-holds-barred dance party (always a hit with the younger kids). Our souls were wired to sing, and our Scriptures command it of us:

> ^{2} *Sing to him, sing praises to him;*
> *tell of all his wondrous works!*
> ^{3} *Glory in his holy name;*
> *let the hearts of those who seek the LORD rejoice!*
> ^{4} *Seek the LORD and his strength;*
> *seek his presence continually! (Psalm 105 v 2-4)*

There are, of course, many other activities you could engage in during your rest. That is part of why it is more of an art and less of an injunction. As you start to stop, you find yourself getting better at it, and getting more out of it.

WHAT ARE YOU GOING TO DO NOW?

So there you have it: a blueprint for a break from all your busyness. The only remaining thing to do now (apart from reading the next, last, chapter) is to embrace this new, and perhaps strange, art form.

Hopefully, the whys of rest have become clear. Our culture won't stop working, and the false gods it worships won't stop demanding. Yet we've been given a much different and better story.

God built restfulness into the world on the seventh day.

God defeated Pharaoh, who demanded God's enslaved people work ceaselessly.

God came in the person of Jesus so that we could put down our blessing-seeking work and know that we are forgiven by him—and not just forgiven, but also filled by his Spirit and welcomed into his family.

God invited us, heavy-laden as we are by religious rules and by rebellious running, to come to him for rest.

That invitation has been answered by countless millions from different tribes, languages, races, and tax brackets. And it's that invitation that every Christian has accepted, and that every Christian enjoys as we learn to rest.

So, what are you going to do now?

You could put this book down at the end of the next chapter and walk away. We've all done that with sermons.

"That was pretty good," we thought.

"I should do something about that," we thought.

But by the end of Sunday dinner we'd forgotten all about it. That is certainly one option here.

But there remains another option: to embrace the art of rest. To put into practice some of these small changes. To have a change of mind and heart, and see that God is inviting you toward him. You may just have to stop working for a bit to answer the invitation. It's risky. It may mean less money, or a missed opportunity. It may mean an older car or fewer lattes. It could involve reducing the number of activities the kids do, exposing you to the judgment of others. But I'm convinced that the risk is worth the reward. Hopefully, you're convinced, too.

Time, and how you spend it, will tell.

It will tell whether you really trust that rest brings reward.

And, as we'll see as we finish, it will tell whether heaven is really something you desire.

OUTRO: LESSONS LEARNED IN FLORIDA

*"The world is at present in a mighty hurry, and
being in many places cut off from all foundations of
steadfastness, it makes the minds of men giddy with its
revolutions, or disorderly in the expectations of them …
Hence men walk and talk as if the world were all, when
comparatively it is nothing."*
John Owen, 1681

I grew up in sunny Florida. Which, as I look back on it, is a bit of a strange place. It wasn't the locals who made it strange—it was the guests.

There are two kinds of people who come to Florida: people on vacation and people starting their retirement. Part of Florida is nothing but resorts, t-shirt shops, theme parks, and restaurants. This part caters for the tourists. The other part is gated communities, boat and luxury car dealerships, and golf courses. This part caters for the retirees. These two crowds don't usually cross paths much, but one thing unites them: they're both looking for rest.

Starting out in life in a place where a lot of other people want to end up has afforded me an interesting perspective on rest. Many of my neighbors were millionaire retirees—and it turns out that if you spend a life over-working, you spend a retirement over-boating, over-eating, and overplaying golf. Perhaps it's because the quiet murmur of self-reproach still needs drowning out. Many of the retirees, having burned through their first family while striving for early retirement, would say, in quieter moments, that they regret it. Many, in their quieter moments, may wonder whether it was really all worth it.

And then just down the coast were the tourists, digging into debt to live the beach dream for a week of leave burned by the sun's rays, bewildered that their imperfect kids remained frustratingly imperfect while their parents were trying to relax, and deep down bemused that it turned out Florida isn't heaven, even as they booked up the same place for their vacation next year.

I've seen the end of the over-worked, under-rested life and I'm here to tell you, definitively—it's not worth it.

What a monumental tragedy. We work 50-hour weeks for 50 years of our lives only find that at the end of all our efforts we have earned the right to... play golf? Vacation?

Eat out more often? To suffer with overworked bodies and underdeveloped souls in the golden years of our lives seems like an irony and a tragedy the likes of which makes hell chuckle and heaven mourn.

But this is how the world works—literally. And we Christians live in this ocean of overwork, and so without knowing it we swim with its tides. We labor for that which cannot last only to rest in that which cannot satisfy.

A world that demands endless work makes humans who understandably want to escape such slavery, even if only for a moment. So we spend countless thousands of dollars dragging ourselves to places like Florida to taste—briefly and at great personal cost—a pale imitation of something that resembles a vague image of heaven.

We Christians simply don't have to live this way.

In Christ, we are being remade for another world—a world of meaningful work and refreshing rest. For Jesus' people, the future is neither workless, luxurious self-indulgence nor a laborious, hurried heaven. It will be different and better than both.

A FUTURE TO REST FOR

How we rest in this life reveals what we hope for in the next. Which suggests that not too many of my fellow Americans are hoping for long-term fellowship with Christ and meaningful labor on earth quite as much as they are for a boat, good laughs, and a nice home on a golf course in which to grow old and eventually die. Fun is fun, but fun is fleeting. The future world that God is bringing is so much more than fun. It's meaningful and rich, full of calling and calm. It's a world of work and rest.

The author of Genesis tells us that, after the floodwaters receded and Noah and his family emerged from the ark, God made a promise:

> While the earth remains, seedtime and harvest, cold and heat, summer and winter, day and night, shall not cease. (Genesis 8 v 22)

In other words, the seasonal order of work (sowing seeds and harvesting the fruit) all across the year would never, ever stop. Nothing would interrupt this natural order, because God made a covenant promise to keep life moving in this ordered way.

While it is good to know that we don't have to worry about a global flood, the news that the work of sowing and reaping (or in our case, constant labor to feed ourselves and our loved ones, and meet our needs) might not feel so good. We want a break from the cycle of paycheck and pay-outs, from the clock-in-clock-out monotony. This is why Western culture builds in vacations to break up the work, and retirement as the great eschatological goal of all those late nights, missed dinners, days of anxious toil, and months of laborious drudgery. But our God points us forward to something far better:

¹ Then [says the apostle John] I saw a new heaven and a new earth, for the first heaven and the first earth had passed away, and the sea was no more. ² And I saw the holy city, new Jerusalem, coming down out of heaven from God ...

²² And I saw no temple in the city, for its temple is the Lord God the Almighty and the Lamb. ²³ And the city has no need of sun or moon to shine on it, for the glory of God gives it light, and its lamp is the Lamb. ²⁴ By its light will the nations walk, and the kings of the earth will bring their glory into it, ²⁵ and its gates will never be shut by day—and there will be no night there.

(Revelation 21 v 1-2, 22-25)

So what, finally, interrupts the seasonal cycle of work with its endless (and sometimes monotonous) march?

The renewal of the earth.

John's visionary description of the future of God's people in God's world interrupts the normal rhythms of life—but not in the ways we might expect. If you ask most Christians, they'll probably describe heaven as a place of eternal rest, where streets are paved with gold, we all get a mansion, and we can finally take it slow and luxuriate. A brighter Florida, basically. After all, don't most tombstones say, "Rest in Peace"?

But surprisingly, John describes our eschatological destination not as an eternal retirement community but a bustling city. God, in full and unmitigated glorious presence, takes up residence in a remade world with kings (governance of some sort), open gates (traffic and human movement), and global unity around the worship of the Lamb, the crucified and risen and reigning Lord Jesus. This city seems to be the full literal fulfillment of the original command to the first humans to start with a garden and create civilization.

There, we will experience rest-in-work. Because meaningful labor is an intrinsic part of our purpose (Genesis 1 v 28), our forever future will certainly involve it. But in work, there will be rest. John saw the coming kingdom as a city, and cities are filled with activity, vocation, meaningful labor, and human relationships.

How does rest-in-work feel? The joy of a job well done, of a garden well tended, of a budget balancing, of a symphony well composed, and the satisfied exhalation which follows—can you imagine it? Can you picture, even for a moment, your Father peering over your shoulder as you labor in a heavenly vocation, smiling at your effort. You pause, pleased with his smile in your doings. That's rest-in-work.

But our heavenly future won't be all work, of course. After all, our time there will kick off with the great "marriage supper of the Lamb" (Revelation 19 v 9)—a great celebratory banquet. We will gather to praise the Lamb, around his throne: a great multitude of every tribe and tongue, praising him face to face with no sin to compromise our thoughts or stymie our songs. I imagine that will be really quite awesome, right?

I can imagine our work being interrupted with a restful indulgence in God, laughter with friends, the enjoyment of a renewed world. Can you imagine that? A nap that truly refreshed? A day at the beach that does more for the soul than the most well-padded retirement could ever offer? A meal with friends that refreshed more than the finest fare we can find here? Our rest-in-work will regularly be punctuated by rest-from-work. There, the art of rest will be perfected.

Since this rest-from-work will certainly mark our future, shouldn't it mark us now?

Rest is a gift—a gift where we can begin to taste the thing for which we were made.

Rest is art—an expressive form of the personal experience of rest in King Jesus. It has power both to reveal and reshape. It lays bare our biggest hopes and solidifies our truest longings.

Rest is faith—hitting pause in a world that never stops because we know this world is not the one we were made for.

REHEARSE THE HEAVENLY ART

We were taught by Jesus to pray, "Your kingdom come..." (Luke 11 v 2). Every time we pray that, we're not only saying, "Jesus, please hurry up and come back," but also,

"Jesus, let the culture, customs, values, and practices you are going to bring invade my life right now, undermine my unbelief, and set me free to live with you as King."

When we say, "Your kingdom come," we are praying for God's already-but-not-yet kingdom to be more already and less not-yet.

And since rest-in-work and rest-from-work is going to mark the kingdom that will one day come fully, we can begin to rehearse and enjoy and benefit from this heavenward art now—in part, yes, but increasingly.

The space afforded us by living out the art of rest-from-work gives us a chance to relate to God in ways we can't when we're working. I love taking my children with me when I'm about my daily business—I take them to work, on runs, even on trips. What's more, they love it too. (In fact, they love it so much they sometimes argue over whose turn it happens to be.) But having my kids in my hip pocket as I do things is different than daddy-daughter or daddy-dude dates (forgive me, we pastors do love to alliterate). On those precious evenings, I'm completely focused on just one of them. I hear things from them I'd never normally hear. I say things to them I can't often say.

Real relationships require this kind of restful space to grow. So it is with God. We can find rest with him in our work and rest with him from our work. Our great

Father loves to work with us, and he invites us to work with him here, in the real world. Yet he also invites us to enjoy rest from work with him—simply and purely to enjoy him.

Whole hours spent talking with God can't happen if our schedules are stuffed. If we will create the space, God will speak to us, minister to us, and refresh us in ways we just can't get in our quick-daily-devotional, pray-on-the-way pace of life.

We are supposed to believe in a God who is our sovereign Savior, not our slave-driver; and in a future world where burnout is excluded, anxiety is a thing read about in a museum, and stress is no longer a useful word. We could live out this rest-chatological vision of that future in the presence of that God today if we chose.

What if mom were satisfied enough in God to respond to her kids with more grace?

What if dad were rested in the Spirit sufficiently to face his wife with soft strength instead of reactive angst?

What kind of experience of church could we create if we just stopped all the programs for a moment long enough to learn what "Come to me and I will give you rest" really means?

All work and no rest makes Christians idiots—forgetful children who work like slaves, forgetting that their Father owns the world and they get to inherit it. When we give ourselves the time and space to do so, daydreaming of a day off in the midst of our toil will give way to imagining our everlasting life with God. So daily, weekly, and yearly, enter into that temple of time to be with him.

EVANGELISTIC REST

If we are serious about evangelism, we will get serious about rest.

Can you imagine a church which said no to the stressed-out stereotype of Western cultural life? With deep peace and triumphant tranquility, what a blessing we could be. If we begin to embrace a renewed Sabbath—a time of rest, holy to the Lord—we might achieve both a level of personal holiness and missionary effectiveness not seen for ages past. If we repent of our human-centric, self-reliant belief that more programs, more volunteering, and more activity is always the answer to the problems of ministry and the challenge of evangelism... if we change our view on the necessity of doing every conceivable activity for our children... if we resist the siren call of a better lifestyle at the cost of more of our actual lives... what good could we actually be.

Taking a day off might just be the most missionally effective thing some of us could ever do. Creating a heavenly culture in our homes, our marriages, our children, and our churches could just create a compelling enough counter-culture for the not-yet-believing world to come and see something they may just actually want.

We could embody the peace of God on offer in the gospel by embracing the art of rest.

It's not enough to tell people about heaven; they want to see it. If you and I are serious about providing a compelling alternative to Western, secular workaholism, maybe we need to live one out as well as talk about it—and that means enjoying real rest.

HARD WORK AND HAPPY REST

So, to the stressed-out mom and the beaten-up brother, to the crumbling volunteer and the anxiously overwrought worker, to the pastor who thinks the key is always doing more and the Christian who struggles to stop, come with me. I'm imperfect at this art, but I'm convinced it's important. Like a child learning the violin, I'm going to keep picking up the bow, tuning the strings, and learning to love this strange new feeling of restfulness. Why? Because practice makes better.

I know that it is hard.

I know life is demanding, but it's also worth living.

Rest is a gift from the Father, renewed by the Son, and sustained by the Spirit. So let's learn to celebrate his work as we regularly rehearse the art of rest. Let's learn to hit pause because we have faith.

I'm not perfect at rest. I suppose I won't be until that great final day. But I want so much to live now in rehearsal for the world's renewal—with hard work and happy rest.

The same grace that saved us for God's coming future is available now to save us from our anxious toil. And as with all grace, we can't work for it, but we can receive it.

Trust me—better yet, trust him—there is grace for you in the art of rest.

BIBLIOGRAPHY

Walter Brueggemann, *Sabbath as Resistance: Saying No to the Culture of Now* (Westminster John Knox Press, 2014)

C.S. Lewis, *The Screwtape Letters* (HarperOne: reprint edition, 2015)

Arnold Kling, *The Three Languages of Politics: Talking Across the Political Divides* (Cato Institute, 2017; first edition self-published, 2013)

Peter Scazzero, *Emotionally Healthy Spirituality: It's Impossible to be Spiritually Mature, While Remaining Emotionally Immature* (Zondervan, 2014)

Judith Shulevitz, *The Sabbath World: Glimpses of a Different Order of Time* (Random House, 2010)

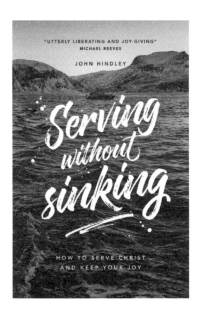

Many of us are serving, and feel we're sinking. We feel joyless, weary, and burdened. John Hindley shows how Jesus was telling the truth when he offered an "easy yoke"—a way of serving that is joyful. Discover why serving is so often joyless—and how our identity in Christ changes everything.

 There is something in this book for every Christian at every stage of life. One of the books of the year.

Christopher Ash

thegoodbook.co.uk | .com / serving

thegoodbook
COMPANY

BIBLICAL | RELEVANT | ACCESSIBLE

At The Good Book Company, we are dedicated to helping Christians and local churches grow. We believe that God's growth process always starts with hearing clearly what he has said to us through his timeless word—the Bible.

Ever since we opened our doors in 1991, we have been striving to produce resources that honor God in the way the Bible is used. We have grown to become an international provider of user-friendly resources to the Christian community, with believers of all backgrounds and denominations using our Bible studies, books, evangelistic resources, DVD-based courses, and training events.

We want to equip ordinary Christians to live for Christ day by day, and churches to grow in their knowledge of God, their love for one another, and the effectiveness of their outreach.

Call us for a discussion of your needs or visit one of our local websites for more information on the resources and services we provide.

Your friends at The Good Book Company

NORTH AMERICA thegoodbook.com 866 244 2165
UK & EUROPE   thegoodbook.co.uk   0333 123 0880
AUSTRALIA   thegoodbook.com.au   (02) 9564 3555
NEW ZEALAND   thegoodbook.co.nz   (+64) 3 343 2463

 WWW.CHRISTIANITYEXPLORED.ORG
Our partner site is a great place for those exploring the Christian faith, with a clear explanation of the good news, powerful testimonies and answers to difficult questions.